The Sol Plaatje European Union
Poetry Anthology

Vol XI

The Sol Plaatje European Union Poetry Anthology

Volume XI

Selected by Mongane Wally Serote,
Goodenough Mashego, Pieter Odendaal,
Innocentia Mhlambi, Neo Sehlahla
& Sandile Ngidi

The views and opinions expressed in this publication are not necessarily those of the funder.

First published by Jacana Media (Pty) Ltd in 2022

10 Orange Street
Sunnyside
Auckland Park 2092
South Africa
+2711 628 3200
www.jacana.co.za

© Individual contributers, 2022
All rights reserved.

Cover photograph: Phantsi komthunzi, Réunion, 2018 © Jabulani Dhlamini
Courtesy of Jabulani Dhlamini and Goodman Gallery (Cape Town, Johannesburg, London)

ISBN 978-1-4314-3292-9

Set in Ehrhardt 11/13pt
Printed and bound by Creda Communications, Cape Town
Job no. 003804

See a complete list of Jacana titles at www.jacana.co.za

Contents

Message from the Sponsor *EU Ambassador to South Africa,*
   Sandra Kramer.. xiii
Foreword *Dr Mongane Wally Serote* xv

Ode to Ingrid Jonker *Ashley Allard*.......................... 1
Umama kaMama, *Ayanda Billie* 4
My Mother's Mother, *an English translation by*
   Innocentia Mhlambi 5
Uyephi, *Ayanda Billie*... 6
Where is She?, *an English translation by Innocentia Mhlambi*..... 7
Os Lewe, *Toroga Denver Breda*.............................. 8
Sada Ûib, *a Khoisan translation by Fredericka Vogelsang*......... 9
We're Alive, *an English translation by Pieter Odendaal* 10
|Uba te, *Toroga Denver Breda*................................ 11
|Uba te, *a Khoisan translation by Fredericka Vogelsang*......... 12
|Uba te, *an English translation by Pieter Odendaal* 13
Mbalenhle *Bruce Sabelo Buthelezi*........................... 14
Beautiful Flower, *an English translation by Innocentia Mhlambi* .. 16
Uhambo, *Nompilo Cele* 18
A journey, *an English translation by Innocentia Mhlambi* 19
Uitstkeityd, *Corné Elizabeth Coetzee*........................ 20
Checkout time, *an English translation by Pieter Odendaal* 21
Don't dala, *Jerome Coetzee* 22
Don't dala, *an English translation by Pieter Odendaal* 23
Hiraeth, *Jerome Coetzee* 24
Hiraeth, *an English translation by Pieter Odendaal* 25
Ma ek is orraait my Lanie, *Jeremy Peter Dames* 26
But I am alright, my Lanie, *an English translation*
   by Pieter Odendaal 28

Basterkind, *Sydney Abraham Davis* 30

Bastard child, *an English translation by Pieter Odendaal* 32

Ode aan Diana Ferrus, *Sydney Abraham Davis* 34

Ode to Diana Ferrus, *an English translation by Pieter Odendaal* 35

Izihlobo Zokukhula, *Sihle Dolophini* 36

Childhood Friends, *an English translation by Innocentia Mhlambi* 39

Fistful of Shells *Hana Nel Gammon* 42

Le Nkondlo, *Martha Hadebe* 44

This Poem, *an English translation by Innocentia Mhlambi* 46

cruising observatory, cape town, *Shane van der Hoven* 48

Umfelokazi, *Sthembile Thingo Gwala* 50

The Widow, *an English translation by Innocentia Mhlambi* 52

Uxinizelelo Lwengqondo, *Anathi Jonase* 54

Depression (Mental health), *an English translation by Innocentia Mhlambi* 56

Apho ndisuka khona, *Sive Joyi* 58

Where I Am From, *an English translation by Innocentia Mhlambi* 59

Toemaar die witman, *Lynthia Arlene Julius* 60

Hush now, the white man, *an English translation by Pieter Odendaal* 62

Kenneth Kaunda robala, *Kabelo Duncan Kgatea* 64

Rest in peace Kenneth Kaunda, *an English translation by Goodenough Mashego* 65

Robala Tshekiso Solomon Plaatje 29 Seetebosigo 1932, *Kabelo Duncan Kgatea* 66

Rest Tshekiso Solomon Plaatje 29 June 1932, *an English translation by Goodenough Mashego* 68

Hopolang batjha ba 1976, *Mpho Peter Khoarai* 70

Remember the youth of 1976, *an English translation by*

Goodenough Mashego 71

Ulala ephenduka, *Nosipho Samanta Khuzwayo* 72

S/He sleeps, *an English translation by Innocentia Mhlambi* 73

Iingcinga zam zindikhohlakalele, *Hleze Welsh Kunju* 74

My thoughts are cruel to me, *an English translation by Innocentia Mhlambi* 76

Bophelo ha se botsole boswetu, *Ntaoleng Patience Labane*....... 78

Life is not black and white, *an English translation by Goodenough Mashego* 80

Fetolang Mawa, *Mmakgotso Annastacia Lehola*............... 81

Change Goal Posts, *an English translation by Goodenough Mashego* 83

Ingelêde perskes, *Keith Oliver Lewis*....................... 85

Bottled peaches, *an English translation by Pieter Odendaal*...... 86

reenboogkruise, *Keith Oliver Lewis*....................... 87

rainbow crosses, *an English translation by Pieter Odendaal*...... 90

somersaults en synchronised death, *Keith Oliver Lewis* 93

somersaults and synchronised death, *an English translation by Pieter Odendaal* 94

Insengwakazi Yenkululeko, *Nkosinathi Emmanuel Luthuli* 95

The Dairy Cow of Freedom, *an English translation by Innocentia Mhlambi* 97

Ubomi, *Nonceba Mabena* 99

Life, *an English translation by Innocentia Mhlambi* 101

Imfundo, *Nonceba Mabena* 106

Education, *an English translation by Innocentia Mhlambi* 104

Uthando, *Nonceba Mabena*.............................. 106

Love, *an English translation by Innocentia Mhlambi* 108

Imazi Emibele Mide, *Landisile Magwaxaza* 109

Long breasted matriarch, *an English translation by Innocentia Mhlambi* 111

Ulwimi Lakho Luyanambitheka, *Landisile Magwaxaza* 113

Your Language is Beautiful, *an English translation by Innocentia Mhlambi* 115

iVulamlomo and the forgotten etiquette *Nolwazi Mbali Mahlangu* 117

Ikhiwane Elihle, *Xolisile Mbali Mabaso* 118

The Beautiful Fig, *an English translation by Innocentia Mhlambi* 119

Esicongweni, *Given Sibusiso Majola* 121

At the Pinnacle, *an English translation by Innocentia Mhlambi* .. 123

Ke sa gopola, *Tshepiso Makgoloane* 125

I remember, *an English translation by Goodenough Mashego* 127

O fetotše!, *Charles Julie Makofane* 129

You responded!, *an English translation by Goodenough Mashego* . 131

Dialila o kae?, *Charles Julie Makofane*..................... 133

Where are bad omens? *an English translation by Goodenough Mashego* 134

Kungusizi *Mbali Malimela* 135

It is sorrow *an English translation by Innocentia Mhlambi* 136

Isandla, *Nangamso Malu* 137

The Hand, *an English translation by Innocentia Mhlambi* 138

Home *Susan Clare Mann* 139

Tshomo, *Norman Marapo* 140

Mystery, *an English translation by Goodenough Mashego* 141

Pad, *Marieta McGrath* 142

Path, *an English translation by Pieter Odendaal* 143

Off-grid, *Marieta McGrath*............................... 144

Off-grid, *an English translation by Pieter Odendaal*........... 146

Burnt Orange *Frank Meintjies* 148

Ubhubhane weKhovithi, *Phindile Memani* 150

Covid Pandemic, *an English translation by Innocentia Mhlambi* 151

Dlal'uhadi, *Tlotlisang David Mhlambiso* 152

Play the Harp, *an English translation by Innocentia Mhlambi* ... 154

Ntinga-Mbhali, *Tlotlisang David Mhlambiso* 156

Fly author, *an English translation by Innocentia Mhlambi* 157

Akekho ozokulwela, *Hlengiwe Mnyandu* 158

There is no one to fight for you, *an English translation by Innocentia Mhlambi* 159

Mina Bengithi Maluju, *Charity Baphakamile Mnyandu* 160

I am calling for truce, *an English translation by Innocentia Mhlambi* 162

Moswa ke a lla, *Mmabore Gladys Mogashoa* 164

A youth's lament, *an English translation by Goodenough Mashego* 167

Loso, *Rebaona Boitumelo Reginah Morule* 170

Death, *an English translation by Goodenough Mashego* 171

Isondo liyajika *Choice Dimakatso Mpanza*................... 172

The wheel turns *an English translation by Innocentia Mhlambi*.. 173

Umlayezo kwaba shonelwe abathandekayo babo, *Simphiwe Mthombeni* 174

A message to the bereaved, *an English translation by Innocentia Mhlambi*... 175

Niwafunani amathala?, *Madoda Ndlakuse*................... 176

Why are you destroying libraries?, *an English translation by Innocentia Mhlambi* 177

Isoshiyal midiya, *Madoda Ndlakuse* 179

Social media, *an English translation by Innocentia Mhlambi* 180

Inyoba ebheka ekufeni, *Madoda Ndlakuse*................... 181

Happiness that is leading to death, *an English translation by Innocentia Mhlambi* 183

Hamba Nami, *Ongeziwe Onge Ndlangisa*................... 185

Accompany Me, *an English translation by Innocentia Mhlambi*.. 187

Nangu uZipho Ezivela kuMdali *Thalente Ndlovu*............. 189

Here is Zipho's gifts that come from the Creator *an English translation by Innocentia Mhlambi* 192

Isibindi, *Lesego Nkosi* 195

Courage, *an English translation by Innocentia Mhlambi* 196

Kwahlongasibi, *Ntobeko Lethu Nkwanyana* 197

At the place of those who will not be faulted, *an English translation by Innocentia Mhlambi* 200

Ibali lami abalazi, *Slindile Nqashi* 203

They Don't Know My Story, *an English translation by Innocentia Mhlambi*.. 205

Isicelo Somntwana, *Zukiswa Zuki Pakama* 207

A Child's Request, *an English translation by Innocentia Mhlambi* 209

Handewas, *Hans Pienaar*................................... 212

Washing hands, *an English translation by Pieter Odendaal* 213

Sunflower smile at the sun, *Ferdie Robert Schaller* 214

Saturday afternoon, *Ferdie Robert Schaller* 215

Khuveth' oluvuth' umlilo, *Bongeka Buhle Selepe* 217

Pandemic that burns wildly, *an English translation by Innocentia Mhlambi*.. 219

Mncedisi Baldwin Shabangu, *Moses Seletiša*................ 221

Mncedisi Baldwin Shabangu, *an English translation by Goodenough Mashego* 223

Se se jeleng rre, *Kagiso Sejamoholo*....................... 225

What took my father, *an English translation by Goodenough Mashego* 227

Ubomi bakho bobethu, *Siwaphiwe Fortune Shweni*........... 229

Your life is our life, *an English translation by Innocentia Mhlambi* 230

Akazazi, *Siwaphiwe Fortune Shweni* 232

He does not know himself, *an English translation by Innocentia Mhlambi*.. 230

Sebalibaleka, *Sithembiso Sibisi* 234

They have been forgotten, *an English translation by Innocentia Mhlambi* 236

Amahlathi Amnyama, *Petros Sipho* 238

Black forests, *an English translation by Innocentia Mhlambi* 240

Umzingisi akanashwa, *Lazola Leon Sukula* 242

He who perseveres has no misfortune, *an English translation by Innocentia Mhlambi* 243

Defiling Stone *Jarred James Thompson* 244

Amagwala, *Mbulelo Tshofela* 247

Cowards, *an English translation by Innocentia Mhlambi*. 249

An Eastern Cape Litany *Crystal Warren* 251

Ndirhalela sikhe sibaliselane, *Zusakhe Rhasatsha Zide* 252

I wrote this for you, *an English translation by Innocentia Mhlambi* 254

Erenkini, *Zusakhe Rhasatsha Zide* 256

At the taxi rank, *an English translation by Innocentia Mhlambi*. . 260

Uyangiholel' emadlelwen' aluhlaza, *Nkululeko Zondi* 265

He leads me to greener pasture, *an English translation by Innocentia Mhlambi* 266

Cabanga, *Lucas Delisiwe Zulu* 267

Think, *an English translation by Innocentia Mhlambi* 268

Biographies 269
What is the European Union? 289

A Message from Sandra Kramer, European Union Ambassador to South Africa

In a world in which the Covid-19 pandemic disrupted and in many cases extinguished a range of wonderful cultural initiatives and activities, I am particularly pleased that this project not only continued, but continued to thrive.

Now in its eleventh edition, this excellent initiative run by the Jacana Literary Foundation continues to celebrate South Africa's multilingual society by inviting the country's poets to submit their work in any of South Africa's eleven official languages.

And submit they did! Many hundreds of poems again swamped the publisher's inbox and the independent panel of judges, headed by South Africa's eminent Poet Laureate, struggle stalwart and healer, Mongane Wally Serote, had their work cut out for them.

Having spent many years working within the European Union's institutions, I have developed a deep appreciation of the value of multi-lingual and multi-cultural environments. They can be an incredible source of original thought, of ingenuity and innovation, of tolerance and sensitivity, and importantly, of excellence. Embracing linguistic and cultural diversity can contribute greatly to the opening up of new horizons for personal as well as professional growth.

By all accounts the European Union is an unparalleled success story in that, despite its origins in war, it has remarkably maintained peace between its now 27 member states since its establishment in 1950. Its institutional framework is without parallel and has inspired in many ways Africa's own African Union. Once again, linguistic and cultural diversity is at the centre of a thriving Union.

Similarly, I believe that linguistic and cultural diversity is one of the keys to a strong and successful South Africa. As the idiom goes: the proof of the pudding is in the eating … so, get yourself a copy of this wonderful anthology and appreciate the diversity South Africa has on offer. It is as vibrant as that found in Europe. It is one of South Africa's building blocks for a better more prosperous future.

Allow me to conclude by paying tribute first and foremost to South Africa's many poets who have taken part in this project. Thank you also to the team at Jacana Media who continue to form the strong backbone of this excellent initiative and to the panel of judges for the many long hours invested in selecting the poems for a marvellous anthology.

Finally, an acknowledgement that it is you – the general public – whose continued support makes the Sol Plaatje European Union Poetry Award and Anthology the success it is today.

Foreword

In the *Sol Plaatje European Union Poetry Anthology, Volume XI* no stone is left unturned. The poets' work, in this culturally diverse and lyrical creative tapestry, turns out to be a poetic reconfiguration of the social circumstance of a nation, are a result of history.

There is nothing there in the thousands of words which is not hand-picked, which is not organized and which is not an attempt at defining their purpose for being on paper. That is because there is a relentless historical and cultural war on the pages of this poetry anthology. The relentlessness has a purpose because matters of life must not and cannot be rudderless. But there is also a possibility of a truce – some peace must exist – because whatever the circumstances, life must be lived in an understood context and must be of quality. What motivates this creativity and recreation in the pages of this anthology seeks to persuade the reader to be enriched by the contradictions of a history of the people of South Africa.

The words that create the poems are themselves shaped by a diversity of languages which emanate from a diversity of cultures and natural resources and express the diverseness of a country boasting a spectacular natural presence: so the poets say.

Even when the poets are brutal because the truth can be brutal, the poets seek to say to the beholder: do not walk away from here without being thoughtful!

Many times when one is stunned by what one is experiencing in the singular and collective expression and presence of the word in this anthology, one will ask, is this poetry? You will, after that question, find out from the creativity of the creatives in this anthology that there are many answers to that question. Here is the soft option of that possibility:

> Just think! How is it to be in the cattle pen
> that does not have a bull you only see
> cows and then calves without pillars
> the wanderer having gone with waste like sorghum seeds
>
> all children need their father
> all fathers need their children
> even the nuns would have loved to have
> first born or last born children
>
> ["…Just think…" the poet demands.]
>
> the bull has been swallowed by the mountain, and calves
> are hiding themselves under their mothers, are cared for
> by their mothers
> the wanderer left a surname without honourific names
> the bull never turned its horns to look back
>
> it planted its mouth in the grass, and simply ate in the veld
> the calves are happy fed fattened in the cattle pen
> with nourished milk with love of the mother
> the wonderer is living large
> the calves and their mother are poor

In this context, the "…bull…", a "…pen…" and the "…cattle…" are not only of an economic or cultural value but a spiritual one also, as in "…Think…". The metaphors leave the subject completely pregnant with meaning. They are loaded with deep and complex meanings including beliefs and faith, not just as simple thoughts and words, but simple in context. The meanings are completely different.

Before any of the beasts – the bull, the cow, the calves – become food, they have a familial link between the living and the ancestors. They are used in rituals. And therefore, they are of high regard culturally and spiritually as they are from a belief system. This must not mean that there is no diversity of culture or belief. The innate diversity of the South African nation is the definition of the South Africanness of being South African.

When a pen is a sacred space and a pen is also an expression of material wealth, the likelihood is that the cows, the calves and the bull, all carry and are loaded differently with value and therefore also treasured in a different manner. That is why we are ordered to "Just think...!"

Life cannot continue without its cycles. No matter the contradictions of and within life, the cycles of life have their own strength and will for continuity. That does not mean that there cannot be ruptures. Ruptures are part of the cycles of life, and are for its sake or are not without a purpose. Is that why the lives of even "...nuns..." have innate value to it even as the reality of the institution of nunnery has different principles as compared with that of blood relations and of a family?

When history is forgotten, the values which define it are neglected and the culture which determine it are obliterated. There comes a time when reality and need for continuity does not exist and will not exist.

> ...the bull has been swallowed by the mountains, and calves
> are hiding themselves under their mother, are cared for

by their mothers
the wanderer left a surname without honourific names
the bull never turned its horns to look back

[The question is, what does a bull use its horns for; but also, how is respect and honor earned?]

it planted its mouth in the grass heap and simply ate in the veld
the calves are happy fed fattened in the cattle pen
the wonderer is living large
the calves and their mother are poor.

And then, the temporariness of life but also the weighty burdens of life yet also the knowing that we are one with the universe and the cosmos and can be so minute and invisible in this context; here is:

Ode to Ingrid Jonker:

i understand
how the crash of the waves
how the caw of birds
flying in perfect formation
how the innate pull of the tide
can be seen as an invitation

how the soapy sea foam
and the deepest blue
are seen as more hospitable
than the shattered mosaic of
fragmented shells
that holds the shape of your foot;

a memory

I understand how the
first kisses of the waves
like your mother
softly lulling you in sleep
make you want to wander
deeper and
deeper
into the icy cold

how the gentle brush of
seaweed and soft scratch
of sea urchins
your final warnings of
do not proceed-
only encourage you
to go further in....

There is a time and a knowledge when death is a saviour; when the need and will to live is no more because nothing matters anymore. Is it the moment when the spirit is most enriched and the flesh is poorer and when the centre of thought cannot hold or is it a moment when the spirit has let go or is perceived to be non-existent?

The poet offers these challenges as choices. The reader may learn and know now that there are moments of choices at times of "...wrestling with the devil..." to borrow Ngugi Wa Thiongo's words. The choices must be made and at that moment, judgement does not matter; what matters then is to be engulfed and be owned by what is chosen.

In this anthology, there are opportunities, which are fenced and therefore prevent choices though, for the crisscrossing of the different cruelties of culture as determined by history. They are expressed not only by language but in cultural acts which carry the power to determine history and as the expression of culture: their softness, hardness, cruelty, awkwardness and then meaninglessness which denudes the essence of life are the subject of the creatives here.

Let's agree with the poet who penned "Bastard Child". That because which nation has not born the "Bastard Child".

> …Today a monument
> celebrates you in Paarl
> with sharp spires
> stretching to heavens
> as if you
> like Jesus
> were created by God himself
>
> Meanwhile your family
> on the Cape Flats wonder
> if you, like Randall
> will come home one day
> before you die

Which spires of the world truly proclaim the freedom of all of humanity? Where? That question must be asked even as we know that all of history ahs forever produced freedom fighters.

The poems do collectively find space to declare this truth.

MONGANE WALLY SEROTE
SEPTEMBER 2022

Ode to Ingrid Jonker

i understand
how the crash of the waves
how the caw of the birds
– flying in perfect formation –
how the innate pull of the tide
can be seen as an invitation.

how the soapy sea foam
and the deepest blue
are seen as more hospitable
than the shattered mosaic of
fragmented
shells
scattered
across
the sand
that holds the shape of your foot;
a memory.

i understand how the
first kisses of the waves
– like your mother
softly lulling you to sleep –
make you want to wander
deeper and
deeper
into the icy cold.

how the gentle brush of

seaweed and soft scratch
of sea urchins
– your final warnings of
do not proceed –
only encourage you
to go further
and further
in.

i understand
why you would choose to
quietly dissolve into
the depths and endlessness,
where you get lost
and forgotten
– floating, suspended –
in the darkest blue

over surviving
in the harsh and sickening and
loud and boisterous
tumultuousness of the
world above the waves
where everyone needs everything constantly
and always and never ever allow you to
just
breathe.

but please don't forget

that, back on the shore,
the sand still holds
the shape of your foot
– a memory –
even if it is just until
the tide comes in.

       ASHLEY ALLARD

Umama kaMama
Xhosa

unomvula ngunomarika
ufunqule ikhaya lakhe
ukhongozele iinyembezi
ngengxowa zetapile neze khaphetshu

umama wakhe
uhleli ngase ziko uzamisa isidudu

umlenze wasekhohlo ezantsi kwedolo
unesilonda esingapholiyo
usithandele ngebhandeji elimhlophe

ebusuku uyagcuma zintlungu
silala ehleli
sivuke emi ngenyawo

ivumba lenyuka ngodonga
amehlo agoso, asongene
umlomo ujijekile, wehla izinchwe
uvalelwe egumbini, ifestile zivaliwe

umbuzo womele kwiphini
-      kutheni enje umama kamama
-      kutheni ungandixelelanga nje.

AYANDA BILLIE

My Mother's Mother

Nomvula is Marika
She is carrying her family
she is collecting tears
with potato and cabbage sacks

her mother
is sitting by the fire mixing isidudu

her left leg below the knee
has a wound that does not heal
she has wrapped the wound in a bandage

at night she squeals in pain
when we sleep she is sitted
when we wake up she is on her feet

the house has a stench
her eyes are squinted and twisted
her mouth is twisted and drooling
she is locked in a room and the windows are closed

the question stands
-      Why is she like this?
-      Why did she not tell me?

Translated from the Xhosa original – **Umama kaMama** *– by Innocentia Mhlambi*

Uyephi
Xhosa

ecaleni kwetyotyombe
abantwana badlala onopopi
babomvu ngebala, inwele ziyephuyephu
owakhe untsundu akana ntloko uhamba ze

amakhwenkwana ahamba ngogaga ayaleqana
isitalato sijikelezwe yingxolo yabantwana
- hayi lazola ndim okhabayo
- sundibamba mani abu
- sapha sapha sapha kum mangqo

ngorhatya,
sirhonorhono isibhakabhaka bubumnyama
ubusuku buzulazula namazwi abantwana
yena yedwa, akagodukanga akabuyanga

kufunyenwe unopopi wakhe
enxityiswe iphepha le niknaks ehlathini.

AYANDA BILLIE

Where is She?

on the side of the shack
children are playing with dolls
they are red in colour, with silky hair
she has a black one which has no head
it is naked

little boys are chasing each other
the street is full of the of the children's noise
-    no, Lazola, it's my turn to kick
-    let go of me Abu
-    give give give me the ball Mangqo

in the evening
the sky is dark
the evening echoes with the voices of children
only she did not go home

she did not return
her doll was found
in a niknaks wrapper
in the forest

Translated from the Xhosa original – Uyephi – *by Innocentia Mhlambi*

Os Lewe
Afrikaans

Os bewe maar os moet vergewe
maar hoe?
As os vergiet het wat it is om te lewe.
Os soek en soek
na wat
niemand wiet.
Niemand os mos vertel
van hoekom die nou.
Os in tronke sonder einde,
in tronke sonder begin.
Maar ons moet vergewe?
Vir wat? vra ek.
Hoe lyk vergewe?
As ons sit in die kak
as ons gly in die kak
as die kak net kak is.
Hoe kan ons vergewe
as os lankal nie meer lewe.

    TOROGA DENVER BREDA

Sada Ûib
Khoisan

Sada ge ra lkhū xawe da ge ni lûba
Xawe mati?
luru da ga o tare e da ra ûiba.
Ôa tsi da ra ôa
Tare i llga,
Khoi i a lū.
Khoi i ge mîba da tama hâ i.
Tare !aroma nesi.
Sada lam e u hâ tama !kho omdi !na,
Tsoa tsoa e u hâ tama !kho om di !na.
Xawe ta ni lûba?
Tare i !aroma? tita ra tî.
lÛbasa mati i?
Xaub !na da ga ‡nû
Xaub !na da ga ‡khiri
Xaub ga xaub lguisa hî o.
Mati da ni lûba
Sada ga !arulî ûi tama i o.

Translated into Khoisan from the Afrikaans original – Os Lewe – *by Fredericka Vogelsang*

We're Alive

We're shaking but we must forgive
but how?
We've forgotten what it's like to be alive.
We search and search
no one knows
what we're searching for.
No one told us
about why this, now.
We're jailed without end
jailed without beginning.
But we must forgive?
'Why?' I ask.
What does forgiveness look like?
If we're sitting in shit
if we're falling in shit
if everything is shit.
How can we forgive
if we haven't been alive for such a long time?

Translated from the Afrikaans original – Os Lewe – *by Pieter Odendaal*

|Uba te
Afrikaans

jammer
lat ekkie sound soos my abogan.
|uba te dat die woorde sukkel op my verkragte tongue.
die witman se woorde soos sandpapier.
My hart weggeskuur
'n Geskuurdery wattie stop.
Van woorde wat net seer maak
soos hulle os seer maak.
|uba te dat ek nie meer myself is,
ek het vergiet wie ek is.
My tong gespyker soos Jesus op sy kruis.
Sy woorde nou my kruis.
En kommiddag sou Ingels ook my tong naai.
My Karoo ma my mos nie Ingels gevoer
maar nou wil almal pretend
want som wil vergiet
dat van ons is die kinders van 'n buitebrief.
Want japie oppie plaas was ons tog almal.
|UBA TE
En nou wat gedoen
met die skade van jou dade.

Toroga Denver Breda

lÛba te
Khoisan

Tā_ta ti_ aboxan khemi lō.
lÛbate mî di lkha ta ra !goma tsâ
Ti lgai!khohe hâ nami.
!Uri khoeb mîdi lgowaxa ǂkhanib khemi.
Ti ǂgaob lnûbe hehâ
lNûhes toa tamas.
Mîdi tsû tsûs lguisa ra hi
llîdi ra tsûtsû da khemi.
lÛbate tita ti tama !khaesa,
lUru ta ge tari ta a !haesa.
Ti nami Jesub khemi ge !gâuhaib ai !gâuhe.
llÎb mîdi ti !gâuhai
Ti lkhis tse!gâllae huri gowab xani xaehe.
Ti ǂnams mamas tita huri gowab lkha ǂûma tama
Xawen hoana ra llî tama !â llîtisen
lnîn ta luru
!augab ǂhanis ôa da a !khaesa.
Japip !garo!as ai dage hoata hâ i
lÛbate
Tsî nesisa matis
Sa ǂoa!nab sa di xun lkha.

Translated into Khoisan from the Afrikaans original – |Uba
te – *by Fredericka Vogelsang*

|Uba te

Sorry
that I don't sound like my abogan.
|uba te that the words struggle on my raped tongue.
The white man's words are sandpaper.
My heart has been scrubbed away,
the scrubbing never stops.
Words that hurt
just like they hurt us.
|uba te that I am no longer myself,
I have forgotten who I am.
My tongue has been crucified like Jesus on his cross.
His words have become my cross.
One day English will also fuck up my tongue.
My Karoo mom didn't feed me English
but now everyone pretends
because some would rather forget
that some of us are children from outside correspondence.
Because all of us were Japies oppie plaas.
|UBA TE
What do we do now
with the damage of your deeds.

Translated from the Afrikaans original – |Uba te *– by Pieter Odendaal*

Mbalenhle
Zulu

Mbalenhle besibaningi sitshala
Ababe tshale emhlabeni owomileyo badumala
Ngokuthi wabekwa emhlabeni onothile lwaqhuma
uhlamvu wavela
Mbalenhle ukuvela kwakho kwaqhubeza injabulo
nothando kuleli khaya
Kusukela ebunganeni waze wafika ebuntombini
Ebuka amaduna zikubhekile izinkunzi
Ukhula belushobodela ngapha na ngapha
Ezinye izitshalo zibuna
Ngomphako wenhlonipho nokuzithoba wama mbali yami
enhle
Mbalenhle njengoba ukhula
Kusazo fika izikhukhula nezivungu vungu
Ungabi nekhanda eliqinile
Uma zifika izivungu vungu zivumele kubengathi
ziyakuthatha kanti cha
Uma kufika izikhukhula, zikhukhula zibheke empumalanga
Ncikela ngaseMpumalanga kube ngathi uyazi landela kanti
cha umile la.
Isihlahla esiphikisana nezikhukhula sizithola sesilele
phansi, hlakanipha.
Mbalenhle fana njengo jika nelanga ulandele ukukhanya
Uma ukukhanya kusithela ugebise ikhanda
Ukhombise inhlonipho ungabheki nangelilodwa
ubumnyama
Ulinde uzithobe kuyoze kuvele futhi ukukhanya
Mbalenhle uma kufika uzamcholo weziyalo
Ubovula amacembe akho ukhongozele

Kuhle kwesi khukhukazi sifukamele
Ngoba ikusasa asilazi
Umawenze njalo uyochamsela amatshwele angasoze azibone
eseyizi khukhukazi ngaphezu kwakho,
Ngoba iziyalo uyobe uzifumbethe.
We Mbalenhle noma sekufika abokuhamba
Bezibiza ngabasem'zini befika nezethembiso zokunotha
Kwabo nobukhulu kwamagceke abo
Ubohamba nabo ubakhombise ubuhle bekhaya osuka kulo.
njengo mlimi ohlakaniphile, ngatshala ngezikhathi,
ngachelela ngesikhathi,
ngahlakula ukhula, isithelo manje sibukwa yizwe,
Mbalenhle ubuhle bakho ngiyaziqgenya ngabo,
ubuhle bakho obezwe.

BRUCE SABELO BUTHELEZI

Beautiful Flower

Mbalenhle we were many that planted
Those who planted on dry land are disappointed
That you were planted on fertile land and the seedling grew
Mbalenhle your birth furthered happiness and love in this home
From when you were a child until now that you are a maiden
Men gazing at you
You grew up while they were gulping up everywhere
Some of the plants decayed
With the provision of respect and humility you remained steadfast my flower
Mbalenhle as you grow up
Floods and tornados will come
Don't be foolhardy
When these tornados come, allow yourself to be carried a lit by them but do stand firm
When floods come, flooding towards the North
Lean towards the North and act as if you are flowing with them but then you were just standing firm.
A tree that argues with floods always finds itself on the ground, be smart.
Mbalenhle be like a sunflower that follows the light
When the light has gone pass just bow your head
Show respect and don't ever look at darkness
Wait humbly the light will come again
Mbalenhle when the hail of instructions comes
Open your leaves and receive
Just like a hen sitting on its eggs
Because the future is not known

When you do that you will hatch chicks that will never see themselves,
As hens above you,
Because you would have carried instructions
Yee Mbalenhle even those the visitors have come
Calling themselves as in-laws promising you wealth
Even the big sizes of their yards
Take them and show them the beauty of the home you come from.
Like a wise farmer, I planted in time, I watered in time,
I weeded out weed, the fruit is now admired by the nation,
Mbalenhle, I take pride in your beauty

Translated from the Zulu original – Mbalenhle – *by Innocentia Mhlambi*

Uhambo
Zulu

Indlela ibukeka salulififi.
Ithibe amathunzi obumnyama okwenkungu.
Iwumnqansa ongaqhwakelwa mbongolo
Lapho kunwampelwa ngenhloso yokuqhwakela.
Kube ikaSikhumba sehlula abeshuki.

Ngokubude bendlela uzobola umphako.
Ziyovuka izimpisi namanqe asehlane.
Ziyobe zihlobe ngeskhumba semvu.
Zikudida udidizele maqede
Qondis'amehlo kwinjongo uphikelele.
Ziqoqe uqine ngedolo,
Ngedolo uguqe ubikele uMdali nabaphansi.
Uhambo lolo….

Amaqhawe onke anqoba ngokulinda.
Amaqhawe onke anqoba ngokubekezela.
Amaqhawe onke ayibamba ishisa
Nawe thatha izikhali ushone empini.
Ikusasa lakho likulindile.
Likufuna uhlome ngazo zonke izikhali.

NOMPILO CELE

A journey

The road ahead looks dim
It is hidden by dark shadows like a fog
It is steep only a donkey can take it
Where the jumping is aimed at getting across
It becomes the skin that failed the tanners

Because of the long road ahead the provision will spoil
The hyenas and vultures of the veld will awaken
They will be covered in the skins of sheep
Confuse you and you become stupid and thereafter
Focus your eyes on aims you are pursuing
Collect yourself and stand firm
Get down on your knees and tell God and ancestors
That is the journey…

All heroes are victorious because they wait
All heroes are victorious because they are patient
All heroes take the hardest side of the battle
You too take your arms and go to war
Your future is waiting for you
It wants you to be armed with all types of armour

Translated from the Zulu original – **Uhambo** – *by Innocentia Mhlambi*

Uitskeityd
Afrikaans

met so baie dood of siek tot sterwens toe
of bang om uit die huise te kom
nie gereed vir die pes wat wandel
of die los koeël êrens in die sagte lyf
en dan, die donkerte

is dit nou stiller in die stad
hoor jy bejaarde straatplatane sug
die doodgewone mossies
die jammerlik brandsiek duiwe, soet en vervelig droef soos vroeër
(die piet-my-vrou helaas is weg of roep 'n ander lied)

hoor jy ook die bloed angstig in jou ore klop
die lug verbete steeds jou bors instroom
en dink jy – en glo halfhartig – die tyd is min, dis haas verby,
so goed soos klaar met ons
en – skepties, terwyl jou arms om jou vou – met my?

wonder jy wat sal jy maak met jou laaste uur
voor jy ook sterwe, dood lê, gans vergaan,
sal jy spyt wees oor gedaan en ongedaan
of reeds voel hoe jy sag word, oplos, uitskei,
en – moenie bang wees nie – in piet-my-vrou, gewone mossie, brandsiek duif en straatplataan
in sonlig sal vertoef.
            Die jaar van die virus

Corné Elizabeth Coetzee

Checkout Time

so much death and dying
and fear of leaving the house
unprepared for the wandering plague
or a loose bullet in a soft body
and then, darkness

the city is quieter now
you can hear the old street plane trees sigh
the common sparrows
the pitifully sick pigeons, sweet and bored to death like always
(the red chested cuckoo is gone or sings another song)

do you also hear the blood anxiously beating in your ears
how the air, determined, streams into your chest
and do you think – half-heartedly believe – that time is short, running out,
that we are basically done for and – skeptically, while you fold your arms around me – what about me?

do you wonder what you'll do with your last hour
before you also pass away, on your back, tired to death,
will you regret what you have done and left undone
or will you soften quickly, dissolve, check out,
and – don't be scared now – linger on in the red chested cuckoo, the common sparrow, the sick pigeon,
the street plane tree and the sunlight.
            The year of the virus

Translated from the Afrikaans original – Uitskeityd – *by Pieter Odendaal*

Don't dala
Afrikaans

Hou op 'dala' of 'vedala' rond
gooi soos dit my naam is,
Dit is geen label nie.
Jy maak dit jou #quote vir kwai lyk
Vir my beteken dit ek kan 'n lyk
wees, van die mes, die skote of
boots teen die gevreet.
Ek is nie special as ek my 5 second
stap doen nie, ek is nie 'n breakthrough nie
Ek is die een wat elke dag struggle
om by te hou met jou brand new car.
Ek mean ma gebed
kan 'n mens net so ver vat.

JEROME COETZEE

Don't dala

Stop throwing 'dala' and 'vedala' around
like it's my name,
It's not a label.
You create your #quote to look cool
To me it means I could be a corpse
from the knife, the shots,
or boots against cheeks.
I'm not special when I do my
5-second step, I am not a breakthrough
I am the one who struggles every day
to keep up with your brand new car.
I mean prayer
can only take you so far.

Translated from the Afrikaans original – Don't dala – *by Pieter Odendaal*

Hiraeth
Afrikaans

Kindjie van die land skud af
die stof van die land
wat jou voorouers beroof
Druk jou voetsole in die sand
Doen die rieldans

Voel die rooi kleigrond
soos dit kraak onder jou
en die raad van jou
voorouers oordra aan jou.

Leeukop wag vir jou om te leer
dat jy, kindjie,
deel is van die land,
'n koninglike priesterdom

Die potte staan gereed, maar onthou
die land is ook siek. Jou voorouers
was nie al juweel wat ontvoer was nie.
die land behoort aan jou
kom neem jou sit plek in
om die vuur en luister
na jou mense se stories.

                          JEROME COETZEE

Hiraeth

Child of the soil, shake
the dust from the earth
that robs your ancestors
Place your soles in the sand
Do the reel dance

Feel the red clay
cracking beneath you
passing on your ancestors'
advice to you.

Leeukop waits for you to learn
that you, my child,
are part of the soil,
a royal priesthood

The pots are ready, but remember
your country is also ill. Your ancestors
weren't the only kidnapped jewels.
The land belongs to you.
Come, take your seat
around the fire and listen
to the stories of your people.

Translated from the Afrikaans original – Hiraeth – *by Pieter Odendaal*

Ma ek is oraait my Lanie
Afrikaans

Vie ouens is net hie onne inne pad geskiet
Twie is pad op, ennie anne twie is hospitaal toe
mettie ambulance
Ma hie wa os is, is net bullet gate
soe os is oraait my Lanie

Die kinnechies loep vannie skool af
En wod gerop van hulle goetes
Deurie gangsters wat hulle eie bloed is
ma os is oraait my Lanie

Die aunty hie onne tienie velchie
Se huis is afgebrant
Ommat sy die poelisse gebel het in nood
Nou is sy oek dood,
ma os is oraait my Lanie

Os hettie altyd kos'ie
Want ek het mossie mee dai job'ie
Al het it min betaal, kon ek my laaities
bederf mette maal,
ma os is oraait my Lanie

My vrou moet vroeg opstaan
En innie donke tienie pad gat staan
Virre taxi, wannie treine wek 'ie
Ma sy, net soes os
Is heeltemal oraait my Lanie

Os bly hie oppie flats
En ken al die ways en hoe dit dala
Os dala, nooit ontevriede
Met dit wat os het kan ôs nog liewe
Soe os is oraait my Lanie

        Jeremy Peter Dames

But I'm okay, my Lanie

Four guys were shot here at the bottom of the road
Two are on their way up, the other two went to hospital
in an ambulance
We're left with only bullet holes
So we're okay, my Lanie

The children walk back from school
They are robbed of their things
By gangsters of their own blood
But we're okay, my Lanie

The aunty's house was burnt down,
The one who lives next to the veld
She called the police in need
She's also dead now,
But we're okay, my Lanie

We don't always have food
Because I've lost that job
Even though it didn't pay well, I could
Spoil my kids with a meal,
But we're okay, my Lanie

My wife wakes up early
To wait in the dark next to the road
For a taxi, because the trains aren't running
But she, like all of us,
Is completely fine, my Lanie

We live here on the flats
We know all the ways and how to dala
We dala, never dissatisfied,
We can live with what we've got
So we're okay, my Lanie

Translated from the Afrikaans original – Ma ek is oraait my Lanie – *by Pieter Odendaal*

Basterkind
Afrikaans

By geboorte het jou wit voorgeslag
jou misken,
oorlat jou Khoi gelaatstrekke
en kroeshare
sigbaar deurgeslaan het;
maar soos jy opgegroot het,
het jy al meer uitgebleik
en kon jy try for white.

Toe het die Regte Afrikaners
 jou geëien;
`n handige pion,
`n woordwragtige wapen
in die stryd om Afrikaner identiteit

Vandag pryk daar vir jou
`n monument in die Paarl
met spitspunte
wat na die hemel reik,
asof jy,
soos Jesus,
   deur God self verwek is.

Meanwhile wonder die
   die familie op die Cape Flats
of jy ook eendag,

soos Randall,
voor jou heengaan
sal hystoe kom.

SYDNEY ABRAHAMS DAVIS

Bastard child

At birth your white ancestors
denied you,
your Khoi features
and kinky hair
came through strong;
but as you grew up,
you became paler
and you could pass for white.

Then the Regte Afrikaners
appropriated you;
a useful pawn,
a damned weapon of speech
in the struggle for Afrikaner identity.

Today a monument
celebrates you in Paarl
with sharp spires
stretching to heaven,
as if you,
like Jesus,
were created by God Himself.

Meanwhile your family
on the Cape Flats wonder
if you, like Randall,

will come home one day
before you die.

Translated from the Afrikaans original – **Basterkind** *– by
Pieter Odendaal*

Ode Aan Diana Ferrus
Afrikaans

Wie sou kon dink
dat jou woorde,
gegiet in vers en rym,
alliterasie en herhaling;
geweek in diepe empatie
vir `n suster-landgenoot
van eeue gelede
– vermeng met Madiba se versoek –
soos Van Wyk Louw se beiteltjie,
`n aardskuddende effek
oor kontinente en lande
en regerings heen sou hê,
om Saartjie se geskende oorskot
op die wieke van die woord
na haar laaste rusplek te begelei...
I've come to take you home.

      SYDNEY ABRAHAM DAVIS

Ode to Diana Ferrus

Who would have thought
that your words, cast in verse and rhyme,
alliteration and repetition;
soaked in deep empathy
for a sister-citizen
centuries ago
 – along with Mandela's request –
would have an earth-shattering effect
across continents, countries and governments
like Van Wyk Louw's small chisel,
would accompany Saartjie's desecrated remains
on the wings of words
to her final resting place…
I've come to take you home.

Translated from the Afrikaans original – **Ode Aan Diana Ferrus** – *by Pieter Odendaal*

Izihlobo Zokukhula
Zulu

Ngokuya besingabantwana.
Sisacing'isibhaka-bhaka sesekwe ziiNtaba.
Ngaphaya kwalaNduli, kuseKapa.

Ngokuya besiyiMithana.
Sisagotywa, Sinqwanqwadwa.
NeeMpahla zokuya eDolophini,
Nezokuhlala ekhaya.
Mna ndibuyiseleni ngokuya…

UTamkhulu wayefudula esiya eNtabeni.
Abophelele ooPlastiki eMahlahleni.
Ukuze siyazi imfuyo ebeyigqibele phi.
Mhla siyile thina ngeMpela'veki.

NgeThuba loMdongwe eNtlanjeni.
Ukuvundisa uMnqanqa eMgqubeni.
Ukubuya uchininika,
Uxweb'emva kwendlebe emlanjeni.
Awubethwanga ndiyeke!
Mna ndibuyiseleni ebuntwaneni.

Ukuthelekiswa ungafuni ngabadala.
Iqhinga lokudlaliswa ukurhweca-rhwecana.
Okuphela ngeMvula yezihlangu, neeMpama.
Ingqondo ezomini ayizikhulelanga.

Imini zokwenza izihlobo.
Izihlobo ezidlule neminyaka.

Ulonwabo olwathutha nobudala.
Ukuntlontana, neziqhulo zobuntwana.
Tshona malanga!
Kum intliziyo seyihleka ekhaya.

Ndisendleleni...
Ndiqhuba lamoto yam yamaphupha yakwa Benz(i).
Ndiguguth'ulwandle elunxwemeni.
Ndicula elagwijo lalisithi "Ujing'eliweni".
Ndoyele nzulu ezingcingeni.

Ngethuba kuvuk'imikhuba yobusela.
Ukuqulela ubukhwenkwe obudala mhla kuguywa.
Ukuqala kwam ukuqatyulwa.
Enyanisweni sasikhula.

Namhla singamadoda amadala.
Adangeleyo, adiniweyo.
Adinwe kukuxananaza kweengxaki,
Imiwewe yamaxethuka asisitheleleneyo.
Kwakunye namangcwaba asijameleyo.

Omnye uhlala kufutshane,
Kodwa impilo uyibuz'exhabashela.
Omnye engcwabeni sele engaphesheya.
Omnye unabantwana ababini,
Kodwa uhlala yedwa.
Omnye notywala waqhubeleka.
Omnye unomfazi uyazishishinela.

Omnye impilo isambhida,
Nangona ubomi buqhubeka.

Siphosethu Phikelela!
Nam ndiyahleka namhlanje xandicinga emva.

                              SIHLE DOLOPHINI

Childhood Friends

Back when we were children
We believed that the sky was supported by mountains
Over the hill was Cape Town

When we were little trees
When we could be bended
We had clothes for town
And clothes for home
Take me back

Grandfather would go to the mountain
And tie plastic bags on tree branches
So we could know where the cows were last
When we went at the end of the week

When we went for the clay in the valleys
Doing the impossible
The back of the ear would be parched
And you will a beating of your life
Take me back to my childhood

Being made to fight by old boys
Made to play a game of tag
That was ended by a rain of shoes and slaps
The mind was immature for those days

Days to make friends
Friends tha have gone with the years
Joy that has been taken away by adulthood

Playing and joking around as children
Gone are those days
My heart is now laughing at home

I am on the road
Driving the car of my dreams a Mercedes Benz
I am driving along the coast
Singing a gwijo "ujing' eliweni"
I am deep in thought

When thoughts of thieving comes
Moving on to be and older boy
The first time I was kissed
Honestly we were still growing up

Today we are grown men
Who are depressed and tired
Who are tired of always wrestling with problems
The hills and mountains are beyond
Graves that are looking at us

One lives near
Another is sickly
One has long passed
One has two children
But sleeps by himself
Another has continued with alcohol
Another has a wife that is running her trade
Another life is still puzzling him

Even if it still goes on

Our gift must come through
I am laughing today when I think back

Translated from the Zulu original – Izihlobo Zokukhula – *by Innocentia Mhlambi*

Fistful of Shells

I stood on the shore at the edge of the blue sea
A fistful of shells I bore clasped in one hand
Thinking I knew the ocean as well as it knew me
I set forth and left naught but prints on the sand

The things that I sought thought that they could elude me
So foolish, I thought as I ducked through the waves
I would comb through the ocean, its secrets, its creatures
I'd find what I sought; I swore I'd have my way

Nobody saw; there was nothing much to see
As I vanished on, past the waves and the spray
The shells I held fast and the current flowed through me
I trudged through the water and off from the bay

And as I paddled on with my fistful of seashells
My hubris was blinding, my ambition fey
And I scarcely noticed the strength of the sea-swell
That twisted the water and tore me away

The wind howled above and the cold bit intensely
I wrestled the water, I struck and I smote
But like Icarus fallen the tide was against me
My fistful of shells only dogged my weak stroke

The wind and the water my scream swiftly smothered
I ducked under once, then again, and then thrice
Myself I had lost on my search for another
The things I had sought now demanded their price

I pictured my bones scattered round by the blue sea
My fist lost all feeling, my head drifted down
Though before I sank, I heard a voice call above me:
"Fear not, my friend, I will not let you drown!"

I remember not much of the boat, nor the trip back
There's little worth telling from what I recall
I seem to remember I showed them my seashells
And we looked to the bay and agreed it looked small

Since then I have clung to the land and have shunned sea
My fistful of shells has been scattered around
Do you think they're still there? Do you think they'd still know me,
The things I had sought that have still not been found?

HANA NEL GAMMON

Le Nkondlo
Zulu

Le nkondlo ayigabe ngazaga
Le nkondl' ayiqhoshi ngazisho
Ngiyaz' abahluzi bazogxeka basho
Abakuthandayo besho nemisho
Yayo engavez' amangwev' obunkondlo.

Le nkondlo ayinabunkondlo,
Inyakazis' inhliziyo eyisigodlo,
Njengoshevu wendal' indlondlo,
Oshesha njengonyazi emithanjeni yegazi,
Lomuntu laph' uphuthuma ukuyomis' inhliziyo,
Mdali, ngicela ingami eyami inhliziyo;
Kodw' ihaye inkondlo yothando nothando lobunkondlo.

Le nkondl' ayinabunkondlo
Enhliziywen' iyizibondlo nesondlo
Semithamb' ephethuk' igazi
Elondla umzimba ngemfudumalo,
Ephaphamis' umzimb' osudedel' amandla.

Le nkondl' ayinamandla
Nabuciko bengqondo nesandla
Sokukhiph' izifengqo ezifingqa
Inkulumo ziyenz' ihlwabuse
Kepha ixox' indaba yenhliziyo
Enezinhlung' eyophay' izula laph' engaziyo.

Le nkondl' ayinabunkenesi bezingwevu nezimpandla,
Ayiphandliwe futhi okwayo okwezandla,

Ezintengezelayo zingenawo awokuzibambel' amandla,
Ithembele kwesikaSomandla isandl' esinamandla
Okuqhelis' ezingayiwa izindodla zezingwadla;
Son' esifinyelela zonk' izinkalo naphansi kweNkandla,
Esinyakazis' izinkubela ngisho phesheya kwezilwandle.

Le nkondl' inezinungu zenhlungu yesizungu,
Ingumbungu wenhliziy' ephethuk' isiphethu sobulawu
BamaLawu angalibal' ukulala emalawini,
Ahlal' esendleleni ezingela izinyamazane,
Kepha le nkondl' izingel' intombazane,
Zanele, ngawe konke kuyobe kwanele;
Ngiyinkondlo engenabuciko,
Ngiyimpil' enemisiko neswel' amasiko,
Ngicel' ukunginik' amaphiko,
Ngindize ngiqonde kuMvelingqangi
Ngidlulis' ubufakazi bobukhona bothando,
Uthand' olungayiding' intando
Kodwa olugqamis' eYakhe intando
Yokuthi uyomthanda; yena akuthobele;
Uthando olume njengomuth'omkhulu,
Ompande zawo zimile emhlabathini
Amakhulu ngamakhulukhulu eminyaka.

Martha Hadebe

This Poem

This poem does not pride itself with proverbs
This poem does not pride itself with sayings
I know critics will dismiss it saying
What they like saying its lines
Does not reveal poetic language.

This poem has no poetics,
That moves the heart that is a palace,
Like poison of the old mamba,
That quickens like lightening in the veins of the blood,
This person here is in a hurry to stop a heart
Creator, I beg my heart does not stop;
But that it sings the poem of love and the love of poetry.

This poem does not have poetics
In the heart it is food and mainenance
Of arteries filled with blood
That feed the body with warmth,
That awakens the body that is shedding energy.

This poem has no power
And expertise of the mind and hand
Of articulating metaphors that abbreviates
Speech and make it facinating
But it tells the story of the heart
That has pains bleeding wandering in places unkown.

This poem lacks wisdom of the old and grey,
It is not blinded but its case is of hands,

That are weak without power to fend for itself,
It is dependent on the hands of Somandla which are powerful
Who removes very big problems;
His hand that reaches all the planes even including Nkandla,
That shakes the injured including those across the oceans.

This poem has areas of pains that cause loneliness,
It is the formless heart teeming with the source of dream root medicine
Of the Khoisan who don't go to sleep in the room
Who are forever on the road hunting game
But this poem is hunting for a girl
Zanele, with you everything will be complete
I am a poem without poetics,
I am a life with cuts and without culture,
I beseech you give me with wings,
So that I can fly away to Mvelingqangi
To show to him evidence of existence of love
Love that does not need a love potion
But which highlights His own love potion
That you will love her; and she will succumb to you;
Love that is steadfast like a big tree
Love with roots that grow into the soil
Hundreds and hundreds of years.

Translated from the Zulu original – Le Nkondlo – *by Innocentia Mhlambi*

cruising observatory, cape town

a garbage truck coughs up the road
between the legs of street lamps
that with just a tad too little shame
greets the early morning workstress
wrinkled eyes dig out the sun
a necklace sweated around the neck
at the stake of a street corner
she tries to bless me with sunnyside-up flowers

i clap my thighs   a naughty mat
throw my neck   a madonna
fingertips slow-dancing like nuns
give an anemic no-thanks

push in the fish hooks of my headphones

every third light metal

eyes   a spare wheel down the street
past a person with helpless underpants
past the burglar bars guarding church windows
there is a mother who licks sleep from her child's eyes
i open my wallet
bury a pigeon in my handkerchief
before my neighbours can eat it

seven close-ests raining under a mattress
i count their breaths
brown cents one by one

i cross the back paw of table mountain
the devil looks out over
the liesbeek smiles
without mouthing
hear
...
Goringhaiqua
!Uriǁ'aekhoe
Goringhaikona
!Uriǁ'aeǁ'ona
Gorachouqua
!Oraǁ'khaukhoe
...
let hair breed through the tar

                SHANE VAN DER HOVEN

Umfelokazi
Zulu

Izwi liphelele ezinyembezini ngikhuluma nenkumbulo
Ebesithole ikhaya emcabangweni
Efika njemvula, inhliziyo idale uchabhayiyane
Ngimuphelezela eyophumula kwelamathongo
Izinhlizyo zilibala ukubeletha unembeza njengosana

Umzimba ngiyowubeka emalibeni
Ukuze nami ngilibale
Ngigqoke ekanokusho inhliziyo
Ngifihle izibazi ngoba anazi
Bengizila ukudla ngikhuleka , ngingakhuleki
Umzimba ukhandleka ngenxa yokungondleki
komphefumulo
Injabulo ilokhu ikhalile ngokulindiswa
Ngime isibindi noma kubinda
Ngifele ngaphakathi kwelikaZulu
Mazulu ngifile ngaphakathi yamukelani umphefumulo
Obekusika, inhliziyo ithathaibeka yakha uthango
Ukuze ibhale inkondlo yomfelokazi ongazilanga

Angizibanga, izwi lingivusa ekufeni
Lingiyala ngokungalibala amasiko
Ngihlabe idlozi ngalithetha
Kodwa zange ngathethelelwa
Obekusika, nongaphandle bekasizwa isililo
Uthando lushiya inhliziyo okwenyama ihlukana
nomphefumulo
Ngalugcina usiko, ngalungcwaba uthando
Kepha nalapho angizilanga

Okwesibani siphelelwe ngamafutha, impilo ibilufifi
Inhlasi yethemba ilokozo
Ngikhwezela ngiwubasa umlilo ukuze kube yikhaya elinemfudumalo
Kodwa nalokho bekumubasela
Ngehlele ngezansi ngiwabhule amalangabu ingonyama ibhodla umlilo
Uthando luyala ukubuyela kwasfuba lusaba umlilo
Ngiqoma lona ulaka lwabaphansi
Ngiyala ukuhlala phansi ngigoyele abafileyo
Nami ngifile
Obekusika, inhliziyo ibithatha ibeka yakha uthango
Ukuze ibhale inkondlo yomfelokazi ongazilanga
Kazi Langa lomphefumulo uyakuwubona yini ukukhanya

STEHMBILE THINGO GWALA

The Widow

The voice got finished in the tears talking to memories
That have found a home in the thoughts
That arrive like rain, and the heart gets afraid
I accompanied him to go rest in the place of the ancestors
Hearts always carrying a conscience like a new born

I put the body at the grave
So that I too can sleep
And wear a new beautiful heart
I have hidden the scars because you do not know
I fasted food praying, but could not pray
The body is worn out because the soul is not nourished
Joy always complained because it was delayed
I stood courageous even though it was difficult
And accepted defeat just like Zulu warriors
Zulus I have died inside receive my soul
That which cut, the heart took to build a wall
So that it writes the poem of the widow who did not mourn

I have not ignored, the voice that woke me from death
Instructing me not to forget tradition
Slaughtering for ancestors and pleading with them
But I was never forgiven
That which cut, even those who were on the outside heard the wailing
Love leaving the heart like the body separating from the soul
I observed tradition, I buried love
But even then I did not mourn

Just like a burner running out of oil, life was dim
The spark of hope lurking
Building up the fire so that the home becomes warm
But even that worsened the fire
I humbled myself, trying to extinguish the flames, the lion spitting fire
Love refuses to go back to the chest it is afraid of the fire
I decide to choose the wrath of the ancestors
I refuse to seat and mourn the dead
I am dead too
That which cut, the heart took it to build a wall
So that it writes the poem of the widow who did not mourn
I wonder if the day will dawn when the soul will see the light

Translated from the Zulu original – **Umfelokazi** – *by Innocentia Mhlambi*

Uxinizelelo lwengqondo
Xhosa

Nank' umxini-ngqondo enqunqela egoqweni exakekisa,
Dyulukudu, engen' emaxhaka waxaba kwincakami yeengcinga,
Wangumqob' ongqongqo eziqamangela ngamatyathanga,
Ngesantya sofudo engangxamanga wazinza etyhudisa.
Sisilo esinyubeleza ngocwangcu singaqondakali,
Ntw' engena ngoqhwanya oku kwesela,
Iphice ingqondo yandule ukuyithimba,
Yenjenjeya ukuyixhonxa iyingcungcuthekisa.
Inene esi sisixutha-ngqondo esingenantanga,
Sifana nqwa nesiba elikhonya umsi liyobisa.

Yinkunz' egquba kugobe ingqondo oku komsenge exhwithwa,
Yingqukuva elunda luxin' umphefumlo wengqondo ibemxinwa,
Ithi yakuba njalo kuphume ubuntu emntwini,
Adlokove abeyindladiya oku kwenja enomgada.

Abe neengcinga zobulwanyana ngenkqu,
Avuthe ngumsindo elawulwa sesi sifo sinzima,
Atsho ngezigqibo ezirhintyelwe yinkohlakalo,
Lumka wena ukufuphi naye walimala gxebe,
Nqanda esi sifo singamoseli kwisihogo sokufa,
Ungalibali ukuthi qwa hleze nawe wonzakale.

Esi isifo sichasene neenkonde neenkondekazi,
Yiwonci evuyelela intsha yakowethu iphela,
Ibhubhisa iintsana zemidaka kowethu iziqwela,
Ishiya imizi yoninzi idandathekile ngamanxeba.
Iguqula ilungisa ilishiye lingumoni,
Uba alikhuphanga mphefumlo lizisuba ubomi.

ANATHI JONASE

Depression (mental health)

Depression is the destructor of all
Confusion causing, armed and coming for our thoughts,
Restrictive and confined
In heavy chains
With the unhurried speed of a tortoise
Causing confusion
It is a beast that moves soundlessly
A thing that enters in silence like a thief
It confuses the mind after it has held it hostage
Then proceeds to torture it
Indeed this is the mind taker that has no equal
It is the same as the burnt feather that howls making you intoxicated

It is a bull that bends a mind into submission like a wattle tree
That has no leaves
It is a bull that smothers the soul of the brain
making it suffocate
Once it is like that then humanity is taken out of a person
And become unruly and wild like a rabid dog

And makes the person behave like an animal
Their anger controlled by this difficult disease
Which results in bad decision making is clouded by cruelty
Be careful you who are close
Prevent this disease from leading them to the hell of death
Do not forget to always keep your eyes open as you might also get hurt

This disease baffles the elders
It is a parasite that is bullying our youth
It is killing our black children
It leaves many homes devastated by the wounds
It makes a believer to become a sinner
If it has not taken a life, it takes its own life

Translated from the Xhosa original – Uxinizelelo Lwengqondo
– by Innocentia Mhlambi

Apho Ndisuka Khona
Xhosa

Apho ndisuka khona indlala isazi nanga magama wokuzalwa.
Isibiza nangeziduko ngoba yazi zonke izizukulwana zekhaya.
Sisonka sethu semihla ngemihla.
Ngumoya esiwuphefumlayo.

Sijwaxwa linxele likaKhetshekile.
Nezikhova zifumene itha ezinokuyinqola.
Nala kati ilele eziko ilwa nembiza ezigcwalayo.
Ayifuni namanzi abilayo.
Le inempilo ezingapha kwethoba,
Kudala siyihlinza apha ekhaya
Siyitya namanqina wayo kodwa iphinde ibuyele apho ihlala khona – Eziko.

Sive Joyi

Where I Am From

Where I am from, hunger knows us even by our birth names.
It calls us even by our clan names as it knows all the great grandchildren of the home.
Hunger is our daily bread.
It is the air we breathe.

We are walloped by Khetshekile's left hand side.
And the owls found a barn with a cart
Even that cat sleeping in the hearth is fighting pots that are filling up.
It does not even want boiling water.
This one has more than nine lives.
We have been skinning it for a long time here at home
We eat it with its hooves but it returns to where it lives – the Hearth.

Translated from the Xhosa original – Apho Ndisuka Khona – by Innocentia Mhlambi

Toemaar die witman
vir Emmett Till
Afrikaans

op die bruin slaggaatpad
van segregasie
die wêreld om
stap 'n witman
'n bolip dun soos die sekelmaan
gal in sy hart
bloed gegiet vir sy oop keelgat
en 'n rug gebuk van die
white man's burden

wat maak hy, suster?
wat maak hy, suster?

hy roep die dood
hy verag die swart
en 'n donker velkeur
se hart wat klop
tok-tok hulle s'n
hy bid toktokkies bring die reën
vir die heersers in sy kring

wat is sy naam, suster?
wat is sy naam, suster?

sy naam is sjuut, kind
sy naam is vat
meneer ons sal nooit vergeet
toe julle ons s'n vat
sy naam is bordjies oralster op

hy is, onse kind
toemaar die witman

suster?
toemaar, Emmett, die witman

    Lynthia Arlene Julius

Hush now, the white man
for Emmett Till

on the brown potholed-road
of segregation
around the earth
a white man walks
his upper lip thin like a crescent moon
gall in his heart
blood spilled for his open throat
and a back bowed down from the
white man's burden

what's he doing, sister?
what's he doing, sister?

he calls on death
he hates the black of night
and the heartbeat
of dark skin
the knock-knock of its beat
he prays to toktokkies for rain
for the rulers in his circle

what's his name, sister?
what's his name, sister?

his name is hush, child
his name is take
sir we will never forget
how you took our things
his name is on signboards everywhere

he is, my child,
hush now, the white man

sister?
hush now, Emmett, the white man

Translated from the Afrikaans original – Toemaar die witman vir Emmett Till – *by Pieter Odendaal*

Kenneth Kaunda robala
Setswana

Go robetse letlapa, go robetse sona senatla tshipi,
Go robetse letlapa tota, go robetse lentswetshipi,
Motshwarateu o golotseng Kenya Bokolonialeng,
Motlhala wa sepolitiki o re o tlogeletse tšhabeng.

Lentswetshipi le paletse bagateledi go ka le thuba,
Kutu ya mokala o oleng ba re e retetse kwa Malawi,
Chiluba o lekile sepolitiki go busetsa mokala Malawi,
MoAforika a sa leleng mokala o montsho o a tuba.

Tshipi e ntsho e e kgaotseng dikgole tsa bokgoba,
Kgaratlhong ya Kenya o itshupile modisa yo mogolo,
Maesemaneng a golola Kenya molwantwamogolo,
Tshipi e ntsho e golotse Aforika naleng tsa bokgoba.

Robala ka pula lebutswapele la politiki ya Aforika,
Basweu ba reteletswe go go bidika lentswetshipi,
Ke seikana se sentshontsho poo ya lentswetshipi,
Robala le Badimong poo e ntshontsho Mo-Aforika.

KABELO DUNCAN KGATEA

Rest in peace Kenneth Kaunda

Here lies a solid rock, an iron-giant is rested,
Here rests a huge boulder, an iron-rock is laid,
A shepherd who freed Kenya from Colonialism,
You left the nation a shining political path.

Iron-rock oppressors failed to crush,
The stump of a giant tree they said was born in Malawi,
In vain Chiluba tried politically to return the tree to Malawi,
An African who does not mourn for the black acacia tree is mentally oppressed

A black iron that broke off the chains of slavery,
In the Kenyan struggle you showed your shepherd spirit,
A great fighter who freed Kenya from the English,
A black iron that feed Africa from the grip of slavery.

Rest in peace first fruit of African politics
Whites failed to conquer you iron-rock
The blackest iron-rock bull,
Rest with the gods black African bull.

Translated from the Setswana original – Kenneth Kaunda robala – *by Goodenough Mashego*

Robala Tshekiso Solomon Plaatje 29 Seetebosigo 1932
Setswana

Robala le Badimo motho wa ga Modiboa,
O dirile go diregile namane ya Modiboa,
Badimo ba ga Modiboa a ba go amogele,
Ammaaruri Aforika le batho ba amogele,
Lala boroko fatshe la gaeno ba le itseetse,
Ammaaruri 1913 lefatshe le ba le itseetse.

Tshekisho Mogodi wena motho wa batho,
Sehuba sa gago se ntshe motho wa batho,
Hunolola pelo Morolong tema o e kgathile,
E saletse rona tshimo, ka wena o e kgathile,
Khumo ya rona, o rile re e epolole mmung,
Ikhutse le fa re phamoletswe ditswammung,
Swa baswing; tshela dipelong tsa batshedi,
Huparela pene, mokwadi ka gale motshedi,
O huparele ditoro tsa go boelwa ke lefatshe.

Sama mmu o ikhutse matsapa Morolong,
O tlogetse tiro ya bosekaphofu Morolong,
Legodimong go khumo go tsene M'rolong,
O lele Tholo Borankurunyane ba jale peo,
Morolong Oo-Modiboa Tholo o jetse peo,
O jetse ya bosekaphofu re tlaa ja logodu,
Nna ka re robala Tholo go setse magodu.

Pula e komakome go tlhoge matlhogela,
Lefatshe le setse ka khumanego re a lela,
A Botebele ga Mbelle ba lebale ditlhogo,
A BooSeleka ba ale phate ba lebale ditlhogo,

Tota re touta, modiri ga se moji Mor'long,
Jwa matsapa a gago boroko ke jwa baswi,
Ee, a re paletse go a agela mosako a moswi.
29-06-1932 naledi ya tsetseregana loaping.

    KABELO DUNCAN KGATEA

Rest Tshekiso Solomon Plaatje 29 June 1932

Rest with the gods son of Modiboa,
You did the deed child of Modiboa,
May the gods of Modiboa welcome you,
May Africa and its people accept,
Rest in peace they took your land,
In 1913 this land was seized.

Tshekiso Mogodi man of the people,
You remain intimate man of the people,
Free your heart Morolong your role you played,
It's left to us, your part is done
You said we should dig our wealth from the land,
Rest even though we have been robbed of our harvest
Die among the dead; live in the hearts of the living
Hold a pen, always a writer
Hold on to dreams of land restitution

Saddle your head and rest Morolong
You left a proud legacy
Heaven is wealthier since you arrived
Admonish Tholo Borankurunyane to sow seeds
Morolong Oo-Modiboa Tholo sowed seeds
A seed of nationalism we will eat stew
I say rest Tholo thieves remain

Let rain fall so new branches can grow
The world is poorer we are crying
May Botebele at Mbelle forget the chiefs
May BooSeleka lay down their mat and forget the chiefs

We repeat, the doer is not the reaper Mor'long
Yours is peaceful sleep
Yes, we failed to honour the words of the deceased
29-06-1932 the star disappeared

Translated from the Setswana original – **Robala Tshekiso Solomon Plaatje 29 Seetebosigo 1932** – *by Goodenough Mashego*

Hopolang batjha ba 1976
Sesotho

Sethunya ho kgabola,
mokgupi ho apoha,
batjha ho baleha.
selemo ke sa mashome a supileng a metso e tshiletseng.
batjha Balwanela ditokelo tsa bona,
thuto ke ya maburu.

Puso ke tshepe,
hodimo ho rena leru le lefubedu,
modumo ke wa sethunya,
ke thibang ka Mona,
thiibang ka mane,
batjha ba lwantsha sethunya ka majwe.

Batjha ba bolawa seka dikokonyana.
bana ba Rantsho bashwa basale banyane, Bashanyana ya eba bahale.
ha jwale batjha ba hana sekolo,
ba hana mahlale,
metseng ya rona ho rena bowatla.
Ana le hopola batjha ba 76?

Ana le hopola Hector Pieterson?
ebang masene le ithute histori ya Lona,
bana ba Basotho
hopolang puso e soto ya apartheid.
Thwa! Thwa! Sethunya ho kgabola,
ha jwale thuto ya ngwana e motsho etshawana le ya lekgowa.

MPHO PETER KHOARAI

Remember the youth of 1976

A gun sounded
The crowd exposed
Youth fled
The year is nineteen seventy six
Youth Freedom fighters for their rights
It's Bantu education

Iron-fisted government
A red cloud hangs in the air
The sound of a gun
It's chaos
Social discord
The youth face to a gun with stones

Youth are killed like ants
Black children mowed down at their prime
Young boys turned heroes
Today youth refuse school,
They reject wisdom
Ignorance reigns in our communities
Do you remember the youth of 1976

Remember Hector Pieterson?
Black children have self-composure and learn Your history
Remember how wretched apartheid government was
Bang! Bang! A gun sounded
Black education is now similar to white's

Translated from the Seostho original – Hopolang batjha ba 1976 – *by Goodenough Mashego*

Ulala Ephenduka
Zulu

Mandla ami okubambelela aseyadedela.
Zimpiko zami zokuk'ndizela ziyachutheka.
Impilo iyaqhubeka.
Umqondo uzokhohlwa uwena,
Amagama awayengichaza angeke esashiwo uwena.
Sengikhathele uwena.
Konke akusavumi, umnyango wokuphuma usubheke wena.
Ungang'bambi ngyeke !
Konke njengamanje akuphele!
Akukho osekusele.
Uhlulekile, manje ususele.
Sekuchithekile, kanti bengigcwele.

NOSIPHO SAMANTA KHUZWAYO

S/He Needs Sleep

My power to hold on is slipping away.
My wings to fly are wearing off.
Life continues.
My mind will forget about you,
Interesting words you used to say will never be said by you.
I am tired of you.
Everything has fallen apart, the exit door is facing you.
Don't touch me, leave me!
Everything right now must come to an end!
There is nothing left.
You have failed, now you have been left behind.
Everything has been spilled, yet I was full.

Translated from the Zulu original – Ulala Ephenduka – *by Innocentia Mhlambi*

iingcinga zam zindikhohlakalele
Xhosa

ndakuvingcelwa ngumvandendwa
ndigutyungelwa bubumnyama
ingqondo iqiniseke ngamaqam
ndiculelwa ziingcinga ....
ndiziva ndingenagalelo eluntwini
ndiziingqweqwe zehagu

unyawo lwamafutha luba shushu
umcephe ndiwucinezele ncwaba
lungcangcazele usiba lusithele
lifudumale igazi, intliziyo ingcwabeke
zikhenkceze iintsimbi zezulu zinqwenisa

• umtha ofudumeleyo uyandikhweba • amahashe amhlophe
ayasondela • amanxeba ayaphola •
ukufa kuyandincumisa
ndakucinga ngokufa:

1. ndiyalibala ngevumba lomleqwa kamama ekhitshini
2. ndiyalibala ngokunyova ibhayisekile nonyana endleleni
3. ndiyalibala ngokudanisa nomathunjana phantsi komthi
4. ndiyalibala ngokudlala umculo nomafungwashe eholweni
5. ndiyalibala ngokudlal' icekwa elwandle nesithathu sam
6. ndiyalibala ngokubukela imidlalo yeqonga nothulisa
7. ndiyalibala ngesacholo neentsimbi zam zesihlahla
8. ndiyalibala ngenqawa yam yokucinga endayinikwa ngutata
9. ndiyalibala ngomsimbithi kamakhulu nengubo ebomvu
10. ndiyalibala ngala mazi inco imithiyo nala nkunzi imzondo
ikhwelayo

11.ndiyalibala ngokudloba kwamatakane namathole enkundleni
12.ndiyalibala ngokuhleka nogxarha nokhwalo kwiincoko zangoMgqibelo
13.ndiyalibala ngesonka esinamaqanda nesoseji kusasa ngeCawa
14.ndiyalibala ngomcimbi wekhaya kule veki izayo nangona ndiyintlabi
15.
21... ndiyancum...
20... ndiyabhud...
18... ndiyalibal...
19...
44. Nayintini, twentiwan...?
33. nd... mna? ... ubani?

ezi ngcinga zindikhohlakalele... zi... m...

HLEZI WELSH KUNJU

My thoughts are cruel to me

when I am overcome with thoughts
I am burdened by darkness
the mind convinced with lies
Thoughts haunting me....
I feel like I have no use to humanity
Like the rinds of a pig

The fat becomes hot
The spoon clenched tightly
The pen shaking and then disappears
Blood becomes warm, and the heart becomes buried
The bells of the heavens ring and give hope

the warm sun's rays beckon me
white horses come closer
wounds are healing
I smile
when I think of death:

I forget about the smell of my mom's free-range chicken in the kitchen
I forget about riding a bicycle with my son on the street
I forget about dancing with my last born under the tree
I forget about playing music with my first-born daughter at the hall
I forget about playing at the beach with my third-born child
I forget watching theatre shows with Thulisa
I forget about my bracelet and other wrist beads
I forget my smoking pipe that my father gave me

I forget about my grandmother's Wesley Church stick and her red tunic
I forget about that pregnant cow and that ox that have mated
I forget about the calves and lambs that run around wildly in the kraal
I forget about laughing with Gxarha and Khwalo in our Saturday conversations
I forget about the bread with eggs and sausage on a Sunday morning
I forget about the ceremony at home this coming weekend even though I will be the one slaughtering

Translated from the Xhosa original – iingcinga zam zindikhohlakalele – *by Innocentia Mhlambi*

Bophelo ha se botsho le bosweu
Sesotho

Na u kile ua shebella palesa e shoa?
Ke lintho tse utloisang bohloko ka ho fetisisa ho li paka
Boima ba yona bo tebisa moya wa hao lemeneng la lefeela
U lakatsa ho ba teng ha e hlile e le taba, ho e thusa ka maqeba le liso, ho tlamisa maqeba a eona.
Hona joale ntho feela eo u ka e etsang ke ho shebella mahlaku a eona a pona butle-butle 'me a oela fatše a tla a amohela hae
U llela mebala e khanyang e ke keng ea hlola e e-ba teng
Le llela dihla tseo le ke keng la di bona
Mahlaseli a letsatsi ha e na ho soasoa le bara bao e ke keng ea ba shebella ba ntse ba hōla
Nakong eo u khutsitseng, ha u ntse u shebile kutu e fokolang e kileng ea tšoara matla le lisele tse phetseng hantle, matsoho a hao a sisinyeha ka mokhoa o sa laoleheng, bokahare ba molomo oa hao boa omella, meokho e phalla fatše, molomo o qala ho thothomela, 'mele oa hao o hlokomela boikutlo bona, pelo ea hao e otla ka potlako le ka potlako, sefahleho sa hao se soeufetse, 'me ho hema ho qala ho utloa eka ke papali.
Ha e sa le ea ho lebella tahlehelo, e mabapi le ho e amohela ha e ntse e atamela monyako: ho isa palesa ea hau hae.
U le mong ka kamoreng ea hau u khumama ka mangole khetlo la pele ho bua le Molimo, empa melomo ea hau ha e tsebe thapelo ea sello, ea ho kopa, ea ho kopa.
Kahoo le uena u llela seo
Ho bohloko ha o se na matla a ho boloka lipalesa le botle botle ba tsona.
Ho li sireletsa mahlokong a lefatse a tetebetsang Ramaseli pelo

Ha o le mosali, o leqeba le sa okeheng fatsheng lena, o phela o qhitsa mali

NTAOLENG PATIENCE LABANE

Life is not black and white

Have you ever watched a flower die?
It's the most painful event to witness
Its weight weighs down your spirit to nothingness
You wish to be there if it's news, to help with its scars and wounds, to dress its wounds
All you can do now is to watch its leaves shrink and fall to the ground to be welcomed home
You cry for its shiny colours that are forever lost
It cries for seasons it will never see
Sunlight it's not a joke and the sons it will never see grow
When you rest, watching a dying stump that once held power and healthy cells, your hands shake uncontrollably, the inside of your mouth dries up, tears fall to the ground, your lips start to tremble, your body feels this emotion, your heartbeat increases, your face ashen, to breath feels like a game.
It's no longer about looking at loss, it's about accepting as it approaches the door: to take your flower home
Alone in your room you kneel for the first time talking to God but your lips can't lament, to beg, to beg
You also cry for that
It's painful when you don't have the power to bury flowers and their beauty.
To protect them from the pain that tears the Creator's heart
As a woman you are a wound that refuses to heal in this world, you always drip blood

Translated from the Sesotho original – Bophelo ha se botsho le bosweu – *by Goodenough Mashego*

Fetolang Mawa
Sesotho

Ke dilemo re kene tokolohong re lokolohile,
Puso ya rona e se dutse sa maratswana,
Batho batsho ba busa ba laela,
Meralo ba e etsa ba be ba e kenye tshebetsong.

Dintle re di bone pusong ya lona ra tsoha molota,
Batho ba fumana ntho tsa mahala bophelo ba tswela pele,
Setjhaba sa bososela sa hloma eka ke yona tokoloho,
Kajeno ke dikgoba ha ba tsebe ho iketsetsa letho ke ntho tsa mahala.

Tsohle tseo le di entseng re a di babatsa le lekile,
La re batho ba ke ba latswe monakaladi wa kebolelwa ba itatswe menwana,
Ba dutse moriting wa tebalo ba re le wele makgwabane,
Dintho ke mantletse-tletse tsohle di fumanwa di tonositse.

Kajeno re wetswe ke koduwa tlhekefetso e iphile matla,
Basadi le bana ke diphofu tsa mantlha ,
Matsoho a sa sebetseng a sebediswa ke diabolosi,
Motho o qetella a etsa mesebetsi ya ramautla hobane ho se seo a se etsang.

Shebang dintho ka mokgwa o mong bahaeso,
Rutang motho ho tshwasa tlhapi le se mo tshwasetse yona,
Batho ba fetohile mehlohlwa-e-rapame yona mekotla e mahlo,
Ke diritsa tse dulang di batla sena le sele empa basa se sebeletsa.

Re kgathetse ke setjhaba sa bo tsoha o je!
Tlohelang ho etsetsa setjhaba ntho tsa mahala le a se holofatsa,
Se feng mesebetsi se nke boikarabelo ba tseo se di hlokang,
Mphemphe e a lapisa motho o kgonwa ke sa hae.

MMAKGOTSO ANNASTACIA LEHOLA

Change Goal Posts

It's been years since we have been liberated
Our government is in charge
Black people are ruling
They make plans and implement them

We have seen beautiful things in your government and felt courageous
People received free things and life went on
The nation smiled thinking it is what liberation is about
Today they are lazy, free things robbed them of the ability to do things for themselves

We are grateful for all you did, you tried
You say people should taste the good life and live easy
They sit under the shade of ignorance saying everything will be given
It's abundance, everything is found for free

Today we are facing difficult times, abuse is our reality
Women and children are the first victims
Lazy hands become tools of the Devil
People end up doing the Devil's work, there's nothing else to do

Let's look at things differently
Teach a man to catch a fish, don't offer them fish
People have become very lazy
Blind people who always demand this and that without having earned it

We are tired of a nation that says 'wake up and eat!'
Stop offering the nation free things, you are creating entitlement
Give us jobs we'll be responsible for our needs
Begging is tiring, let each man eat their sweat

Translated from the Sesotho original – Fetolang Mawa – *by Goodenough Mashego*

Ingelêde perskes
Afrikaans

groom die perske:
vat 'n stywe mes en skeur die skil van haar gesig af
split die vrug in twee vulvae
om dit te ontpit –
laat jou wysvinger die hymen breuk
dwing die neut uit die lubricated vlies
gooi die perskes in 'n kommetjie water om dit te sterilise

laat die stove warm raak tot die temperatuur van 'n man se woede
skink water uit 'n beker en laat dit sink binne die abyss van 'n pot
voeg sewe koppies suiker by om dit soet te maak
roer die liquid totdat die diamantkorrels versag en eventually verdwyn
soes jou emosies, bring die mengsel tot kookpunt.

plaas die verskeurde perskes in die stroop
dit moet so sag raak soos jy eens was
kook vir sewe sweeterige minute
dit is gou verby
net soos hy belowe het
haal dit uit en bottel alles op in flessies
stoor hulle in die donker, tot jy daarvan vergeet.

KEITH OLIVER LEWIS

Bottled Peaches

groom the peach:
take a rigid knife and tear the skin from her face
split the fruit into two vulvae
to seed it –
let your index finger break the hymen
force the nut from the lubricated skin
throw the peaches in a bowl of water to sterilise them

heat the stove to the temperature of a man's rage
pour water from a jug, let it sink into the abyss of a pot
add seven cups of sugar to sweeten it
stir the liquid until the diamond crumbs soften and
eventually disappear
like your emotions, bring the mixture to boiling point

place the torn peaches in the syrup
until they're as soft as you once were
boil for seven sweaty minutes
it doesn't take long
just as he promised
take them out and bottle in small jars
store them in the dark, forget about them

Translated from the Afrikaans original – Ingelêde perskes –
by Pieter Odendaal

reënbooogkruise
Afrikaans

Moeder kon haar net uitken
aan die wolkvormige geboortevlek op haar regterarm

sy het getransformeer

haar rietliggaam kamoefleer met die bleek laken
oor haar ontdooide corpse

haar naels is kaalgatperske rooi
moerbei-gekleurde hare
wat straight hang vanaf haar hoofaltaar tot by haar sleutelbeen
pronk soos elegante gordyne in 'n mansion

Moeder se vratjies verander in 'n moeras
haar uterus soek rou klere binne haar ribbekas
maar 'n klipsteenhart hou wag

Vader weier om te kom kyk
hy speel wegkruipertjie agter bybelverse
sy buffelbek brom in bas:
ek het jou teen dié leefstyl gewaarsku!

Aurora,
jou gunsteling kleur was geel
dit het jou herinner aan soetsalige somermiddae
maar jou begrafnis is geverf in onweer grys
daar was geen kerkdiens
maar ons het jou favourite pinksterkoortjie gesing op pad

na jou ouerhuis:

nuwe mens, nuwe mens
al die ou dinge het verbygegaan
alles het nuut kom word

julle huis is nie 'n metjieboks soos jy dit beskryf het nie
maar dis verstaanbaar
jy was jarelaas hier

die lemoenboom wat jou pa geplant het
dra steeds nie vrugte nie

haar begrafnispamfletjie is 'n eensame   bladsy
wit duiwe koer koersvas om die spasies te vul
onder 'n melktande glimlag in die middel van die pamfletjie
is haar dooie naam geskryf in vloekwoord cursive:
                  nikodemus koopman

sy moes haarself deur die lewe dra,
so dis verstaanbaar dat daar geen pallbearers is nie
sy is gekleed in een van haar pa se stowwerige kerkpakke
'n kaalgeskeerde kroon rus kragteloos op delila kussings
haar kaneelgeel dop is suigelingsag
dis hoe Moeder en Vader haar ken

sy sluimer binne haar hazel houthuis propvol goedkoop ruikers
onbewus van haar ontneemde vroulikheid

Aurora,
toe die teenstanders by die begraafplaas verdwyn
soos die rook van cheap entjies
het ek die naam op jou kruis doodgekrap
nikodemus koopman
met 'n permanent koki het ek jou ewige tuiste versier
met jou regte naam

Aurora Koopman

KEITH OLIVER LEWIS

rainbow crosses

Mother could only identify her
by the cloud-shaped birthmark on her right arm

she has been transformed

her reed body is camouflaged with the pale sheet
over her thawed corpse

her nails are nectarine red
her mulberry-coloured hair
hangs straight from her high altar up to her collarbone
like elegant curtains in a mansion

Mother's warts become a marsh
her uterus wants mourner's clothes in her chest
but a petrified stone heart keeps guard

Father refuses to attend
he plays hide and seek behind bible verses
his buffalo voice grumbles in bass:
I warned you against this lifestyle!

Aurora,
your favourite colour was yellow
it reminded you of sweet, blissful summer afternoons
but your funeral is painted in stormy grey
there was no church service
but we sang your favourite Pentecostal chorus on the way to
your parents' house:

new creation, new creation
all the old things are gone
everything's made new

their house isn't the matchbox you made it out to be
but it's understandable
you haven't been here for years

the orange tree that your father planted
still refuses to carry fruit

her memorial pamphlet is a lonely   page
white doves coo, consistently fill the gaps,
beneath a milk-teeth smile in the middle of the pamphlet
her dead name is written in a cursive cuss:
                nikodemus koopman

she had to carry herself through life,
so the absence of pallbearers is understandable
she is wearing one of her dad's dusty sunday suits
a cleanly shaven crown rests feebly on delila cushions
her cinnamon yellow shell is soft like a baby's
that's how Mother and Father remember her

she sleeps in her hazel house filled with cheap bouquets
unaware that she's been stripped of her womanhood

Aurora,
when the adversaries leave the cemetery

like the smoke from cheap cigarettes
I scratch the name out on your cross
nikodemus koopman
I decorate your resting place with a koki
with your true name

Aurora Koopman

Translated from the Afrikaans original – reënbooogkruise –
by Pieter Odendaal

somersaults en synchronized death
Afrikaans

We play dead. Die coffin waters dra ons corpses soos pallbearers. We levitate. Asof die rivier die caves op ons gesigte oorstroom het, om 'n lake te bou uit longe wat gewoond is om te smeek na asem. I often wonder if it was god that kept our brown bodies buoyant, maar die foxing pages van water archives the true tea. Day one. 'n Somersdag. Liquid braak uit die bek van god en declare: Sonder my kan julle nie lewe nie. Day six. Saterdag. The wake. With limbs that are also dumbbells, sink jou ancestors na die bodem en bou 'n kerk uit debris. God het vergeet hoe om te swem. Anchored to the banks, ons moeders, wading their toes in cloves. Hulle het nooit geleer hoe om te swem nie, maar weet hoe om die voetspore van dood te track op die maroon morgue. They warn us. Die kanoe teer is 'n spy wat al ons geheime aan die estuary spill. Eendag gaan die see – die bloedbad waarop kiste roei – ons terugroep. Die gedreineerde dinge: Ons vaders. Hulle shove geswelde lewers in die orifices van bruin bottels. At the base they find cavities left by their own fathers. They won't mourn us. Ons is brave om dood te mock in die serpent. Kaal kaneel rûe rendered to the sun. Geel gesigte submerged in umber. Elmboë as uitgestrekte vinne. Drywende kranse bo 'n slithering stoet, unaware that dead brown bodies do not float.

KEITH OLIVER LEWIS

somersaults and synchronized death

We play dead. The coffin waters carry our corpses like pallbearers. We levitate. As if the river flooded the caves on our faces to build a lake from lungs that are used to beg for breath. I often wonder if it was god that kept out brown bodies buoyant, but the foxing pages of water archive the true tea. Day one. A summer's day. Liquid vomits from god's mouth and declares: You cannot live without me. Day six. Saturday. The wake. With limbs that are also dumbbells, your ancestors sink to the bottom and build a church from the debris. God has forgotten how to swim. Anchored to the banks, our mothers, wading their toes in cloves. They never learnt to swim, but they know how to track death's footsteps on the maroon morgue. They warn us. The canoe is a spy spilling all our secrets to the estuary. One day the ocean – the bloodbath on which the coffins glide – will call us back. The drained things: our fathers. They shove swollen livers in the orifices of brown bottles. At the base they find cavities left by their own fathers. They won't mourn us. We are brave to mock death in the serpent. Naked cinnamon backs rendered to the sun. Yellow faces submerged in umber. Elbows like outstretched fins. Floating wreaths above a slithering procession, unaware that dead brown bodies do not float.

Translated from the Afrikaans original – somersaults en synchronized death – *by Andre Odendaal*

Insengwakazi Yenkululeko
Zulu

Esanamhlanje asisefani nesasendulo,
Phela sesadlula esobandlululo,
Esakudalo!

Bheka nje naba oNomfundo
Basancela,
Buka nje naba noMfundo
Nabo abazibekile phansi,
 Nabo abayizibile eyemfundo.

Siyancela sonke,
Kukhala ubukleklekle,
Sikleza kweligwansile ibele leli,
Siklezela kwelibanzi ithunga leli,

Futhi siya khona ngokuphangelana,
Nokh' asiphangelan' ngezinkezo,
Siphana ngokwabelana wona
Lo msoco okulel' gula,
Siphana ngokucozulelana wona
Lo msoco okuleli gula.

Nakhu nako-Amahle
Nakhu nakoo–Enzo imbala!
Izinga lithi thuthu usuku nosuku,
Abasathintwa ko-a,e,i,o,u!

Phela nabo abazithelile
Ngabandayo,

Bayancela kuwo
Lo ogwansile umbelekazi,
Kulo elibhonsile ibelekazi
Layo le nsengwakazi.

Ncinci bo!
"Siyabonga siyanconcoza!"
Ziyachichima yinjabulo"
Izinhliziyo zabo,
Bona phela "omawabo"
"Omaka-Enzo" belu!

Namankonyane awazibekile phansi,
Phela ayatshakadula nje!
Ayalibona nalo ibelekazi
Elibhonsile,
Futhi ayawubona nombelekazi
Ogwansile,
Lapho-ke ubisi luyachichima ethungeni,
Chi, chi, chi…

    NKOSINATHI EMMANUEL LUTHULI

The Dairy Cow of Freedom

Today's (schooling) is no longer the same as the one of the past,
We have gone past racial segregation schooling,
It is now the thing of the past!

Look here are Nomfundo and them
They are suckling,
Look here are Mfundo and them
They too are not resting,
They too are not ignoring education.

All of us are suckling,
Only the suckling sounds can be heard,
We are drinking directly from the protruding udder
We are drinking directly from a big milk-pan,

We even go there competing against one another,
Nonetheless, we do not compete about spoons,
We share equally amongst ourselves
The nutrition inside this gourd
We share by splitting it evenly amongst ourselves
This nutrition inside this gourd.

There is Amahle
Here too are Enzo!
The standards increase day by day
They no longer begin with a, e, i. o, u!

They too do not pour down (education)

With cold water
They are suckling from
This udder that is full,
Go for this udder that is protruding
Of this dairy cow

How contenting it is
"We are truly grateful!"
The (children) are full of happiness
Their hearts,
Them, being their "mothers",
"The mothers of Enzo" of course!

The calves are also engaging,
They are running about everywhere!
They too see the big udder
That is protruding,
Again, they see the big udder
That is full
Milk is overflowing from the milk-pan
Chi, chi, chi…

Translated from the Zulu original – Insengwakazi Yenkululeko
– *by Innocentia Mhlambi*

Ubomi
Xhosa

Ubomi luxanduva kumntu wonke
Ubomi bundl'elenyuk'isehla
Ubomi bunamanzithi-nzithi
Ubomi ngumnqantsa ukunyuka
Ubomi yindlel'ende
Maxa wambi bumnandi
Maxa wambi buyahlaba.

Qalisa ngoku ukusebenz'ubeka
Qalisa ngoku ukuty'ugcina
Qalisa ngoku ukuhamb'uphumla
Qalisa ngoku ukutheng'ubeka
Qalisa ngoku ukusebenz'ugoduka
Ngoba ngenye imini…
Ubomi buya kukujikela, ukhalel'intsuku zakho.

Abunantombi, abunamfana
Abunamama, abunatata
Abunaxhegwazana, abunaxhego
Abunamntwana, abunamnt'umdala
Abunasifundiswa, abunamnt'ungafundanga
Abunasityebi, abunahlwempu
Xa bufikile bushiya bubonakala
De maxa wambi uve kusithiwa:
"Kazi umzi owawulapha wayangaphi na?"

Bubomi ke obo,
Bunjalo ke ubomi!
Ubomi luxanduva lwakho

Zilungiselele ngoku, ulungiselela ingomso
Ngoba awazi ingomso likuphatheleni.

Lumka, lumka, lumkel'ubomi!

Nonceba Mabena

Life

Life is a responsibility to everyone
Life has ups and downs
Life has challenges
Life is a steep hill
Life is a long road
At times it is good
At times it is a bed of thorns

Start working now and save
Start now to eat and keep safe
Start now to walk and take a break
Start now to buy and save
Start now to work for going home
Because one day…
Life goes on cry for your days

It does not have a favourite girl and boy
It does not have a favourite father and mother
It does not have a favourite grandmother and grandfather
It does not have a favourite child and an old person
It does not have a favourite educated and illiterate person
It does not have a favourite rich person and poor person
When it has arrived it leaves a mark
At times you will hear people say
"I wonder what happened to my house that was here"

That is life
Life is like this
Life is your responsibility

Start preparing now, for tomorrow
Because you do not know what it has for us

Be aware be aware of life

Translated from the Xhsoa original – **Ubomi** – *by Innocentia Mhlambi*

Imfundo
Xhosa

"Siphe Bawo isonka sethu semihla ngemihla."
Naso ke eso sonka.
Thabatha xa usenethamsanqa lokusiphiwa
Ngoba awulazi ingomso likuphathele ntoni.

Imfundo sisonka sethu semihla ngemihla
Imfundo sisipho esingenakuxhwithwa
Imfundo lilifa ongenakulishiyela nomntwana wakho
Imfundo sisipho sakho
Thatha uval'isandla ufumbathe
Kodwa usisebenzise ngendlela eyiyo.

Baninzi ababesifuna baze abasifumana
Baninzi ababesinxanelwe
Koko wakude umthombo,
Bambi bengenandlela
Bambi bengenabazali
Bambi besonqena isikolo.

Vuya wena ubabaliweyo
Gcoba wena usiphiweyo
Kodwa ungazigwagwisi ngaso
Umkhumbule futhi owayekuphile
Ugqibele ngokusisebenzisa ngendlela.
Ubanike nawe abo basinxanelweyo
Ubacenge ubabonise ukubaluleka kwaso.

"Siphe Bawo isonka sethu semihla ngemihla."

NONCEBA MABENA

Education

"Give us our lord our daily bread."
Here is that bread
Take it while you can
Because you do not know what tomorrow has for you

Education is our daily bread
Education is a gift that will never be taken from you
Education is an inheritance that will never be inherited by your children
Education is your gift
Take it and close your hand tight
But use it the right way

Many have wanted it but never got to have it
Many have thirsted for it
The well has always remained far from them
Some did not have a way
Some did not have not parents
Some were school fearing

Be happy that you were blessed with it
You who have been gifted rejoice
But do not be arrogant about it
Remember the one who gifted it you
And make use of it the right way
And also give it to those who are thirsty for it
Persuade them into seeing its importance

"Give us our Lord our daily bread."

Translated from the Xhsoa original – Imfundo – *by Innocentia Mhlambi*

Uthando
Xhosa

Lumnandi okobusi,
Ukanti lukrakra okwencindi yekhala.
Lunencasa luyanambitheka okweswekile,
Kwalona lumuncu okwelamuni.
Luthando ke olo!

Zonke ezimbi nezintle
Zigcwele kulo.
Konke okubi nokumnandi
Kuqulathwe kulo.
Konke okukrakra nokunencasa
Kufumaneka kulo.

Uthando ngumkhombi wendlela
Ukanti lukwanguye nomlahlekisi.
Uthando ngumthombo wobomi
Ukanti lukwangumtshabalalisi wobomi.
Indlela yalo yigolide
Kanti iyakwazi ukutshintsha ibe nameva.

Xa useluthandweni awulambi awunxanwa
Xa useluthandweni uhlala wonwabile
Xa useluthandweni uhlala ukhululekile
Kodwa lumka lungakujikeli
Ngoba wolamba futhi unxanwe
Uhlale ukhathazekile futhi ungakhululekanga
Ngoba nangona lumnandi nje aluthembekanga.

Luthando ke olo
Lunjalo ke uthando
Lulumkele ngoba nalo likundwebele!

> NONCEBA MABENA

Love

Love gives life
Love builds
You cannot say you love me
When you insult me!

Love opens my eyes
Love shows me
I went astray
In this world
When there is no Love

Stop them! They are fighting
Stop them! They are hurting each other
You cannot say you love me
When you insult me!

Love opens your eyes
Love shows me
I went astray
In this world
When there is no Love

Translated from the Xhsoa original – Ithando – *by Innocentia Mhlambi*

Imazimazi Emibele Mide
Xhosa

TShotsh'ubekho Zwelitsha,
Wena'usiphathel'izintw'ezintsha
Satsho saxhaml'ubom obutsha
Saxhamla sonke kungajongwebala
Kaloku le ntsengwanekazi yeyeSizwe

Nguvimba kwabangathathi ntweni
Kodwa beneminqweno esezinkwenkwezini,
Yitshefu yokwasul'iinyembezi
Kuloo mehlo kade elil'iinyembezi
Ewe le ntsengwanekaz, yeyeSizwe

Zwelitsha uyayithand'imfundo ndikuncamile
Mhla sabuya kwa Zwelidala wasithembisa,
Wath'imfundo izakubanye,
Kwaye sizakuyixhamla kunye
Ngenene ezo zithembiso azibanga lilize,
Nali kalokwi'ilinge lokuxhas'imfundo
Nants'intsengwanekazi yeSizwe

Le mazi isizalel'amaduna namathokazi
Isizalel'abongikazi noogqirha
Yasizalel'amagqwetha neejaji
Yasizalel'iinzululwazi neenjineli
Kungasa ke kambe sibal'amathole walemazi,
Ewe le mazi isizalel' iSizwe madoda.

Zwelitsha unenceba,
Akutsho mna kutshwe'esa sikhwabakazi

Kaloku namhla kweli khaya yimivuyo.
Namhla kwelikhaya sibon'imbunguzulu
Kungenxa yemisebenzi yakho Zwelitsha
Wena kaloku usiphathel'itsengwanekazi
Tshotsh'ubekho Zwelitsha
Ncilili!!!!

    LANDISILE MAGWAXAZA

Long-Breasted Matriarch

Great is the arrival of the new nation
You have come with new things for us
We are now benefiting from the new life
We all benefited and skin colour was not relevant
For this little girl belongs to the nation

It is an obstacle to the ignorant
But they have desires that are in the stars
It is a handkerchief that wipes away tears
To those eyes that were crying tears
Yes this little girl belongs to the nation

New Nation you love education
When we came back from the old nation you promised us
you said that education will become one
Also that we will benefit all
Indeed those promises were not in vain
Here is an effort to support education
Here is the little girl of the nation

It has given birth to males and heifers
It has birthed nurses and doctors
It birthed lawyers and judges
It birthed scientists and engineers
I will count until sunrise talking about the birth lings
Yes, it has birthed the nation

New nation you have mercy
It is not I who says that

Today there is joy in this house
Today in this home we are seeing miracle
It is because of your work Zwelitsha
You have brought us a little girl
Good that you are here Zwelitsha

Translated from the Xhosa original – Imazi Emibele Mide – *by Innocentia Mhlambi*

Ulwimi Lwakho Luyanambitheka
Xhosa

Tyhini! kanene sikhululekile,
Kaloku besikade sibophelelekile
Iilwimi zethu zicinezekile,
Phantsi kolawulo lwengcinezelo zingazelwento
Nathi sigutyungelwa yintandabuzo Safun'kunyevulel'izeseko zobom bethu.

Theth'ulwimi Iwakho mnt'omtsha uzingce.
Luthethe kuba luya nambitheka,
Luthethe uman'ukusifundisa
Kaloku obo buncwane siyabulangazelela.
Ubuncwane beelwimi zeli lizwe
Iilwimi zethu intsika yobuzwe bethu.

Sothulela umnqwazi ulawulo olutsha.
Ulawulo olufike Iweza notshintsho,
Lwafika lwathetha phandle ngelwimi zethu.
Lwafika lwathi zonk'iilwimi ziyalingana.
Zatsho zagqa'ilwimi zethu zagqama
Zagqama zabuyelwa sisidima
kwalani ke ngoku ungatheth'ulwimi Iwakho nje?

Theth'ulwimi lwakho mnt'omtsha.
Qhayisa ngalo kweziny'izizwe
Qhayisa ngalo kuba luyigolide
Igolide eyakhutshwa ebugxwayibeni bengcinezelo
Wafik'uSol Plaatjie namanye amatshantliziyo bayivuthulula
Balwa baxolel'ukujingiliso ngezinto zethu zexabiso
Phakathi kwezo zinto zilwimi zeli lizwe

Theth'ulwimi lwakho ke ngako kuba luyanambitheka.
Zekube njalo!!

                                                                          Landisile Magwaxaza

Your Language is Beautiful

Oh! We are free
We were in shackles
Our languages were oppressed
Under the oppressive regime
We are overwhelmed by doubt, and we want to forsake our foundation.

Speak your language and be proud young person
Speak it because it is beautiful
Speak it and teach us
We long for that treasure
The treasure of our languages
Our languages are a pillar of our nationhood

We take our hats off to the new regime
A regime that came with changes
And it was outspoken about our languages
It said that all the languages are equal
Our languages shone bright
They brightened and got back their dignity
What is stopping you from speaking your language?

Speak your language young person
Boast about it to other nations
Boast about it because it is gold
Gold that was dug up from the filth of oppression
Sol Plaatjie came with others and cleaned it
They fought to the death for the things we valued

Among those things was the languages of this country
Then speak your language because it is beautiful
Let it be like that

Translated from the Xhosa original – Ulwimi Lwakho Luyanambitheka – *by Innocentia Mhlambi*

iVulamlomo and the forgotten etiquette

after countless moons of drought
father dreams an ocean fat with rain
a dust devil ripples into clay
and before dawn cracks
i wade my way to the lake
return shouldering a cow

sometimes dreams are just that;
dreams

by the time i am halfway home
the sun had already started chewing her way upward
from her belly day poured into our kraal

there
mother licking the milky sorghum soft porridge trickling
down her left arm
father carelessly slurping his tea
both on the stoep under the makeshift veranda

i plonked the beast down at my father's feet
it belched and no one found it rude
i cowered beneath its breath
how could they protest with mouths full of food

NOLWAZI MBALI MAHLANGU

Ikhiwane Elihle
Zulu

Themba lami ndodakazi yami Mkhiwane wam omuhle,
Omaqabunga aluhlaza ubusika nehlobo. Qhawekazi lam bengiziqhenya ngawe,
Impela bengingazi ngikhihla isililo sokuphoxeka ngawe
Kuwe bengibona umhlengikazi
Ukukhanya kwalomuzi namhlanje bheka sekuphenduke ize,
Ngangithi mangikuyala mntanami uyangizwa,
Yeka ukukhalipha kwakho mntanami ngangithi uyoba utho ngomuso.
Kodwa namhlanje intendele ibindwe isidwa akusabonakali nokuthi ufundile zibulo lami.
Ukube wangilalela nokungilalela wawaphila amazwi ami ngabe usemadlelo luhlaza,
Ngiyazi mntanami lixhoshwa libhekile kodwa kuwe bengingalindele kuxhopheka ngoba ngangikutshelile.
Namhlanje ubangwa nezibi ukungalaleli kukuholelile,
Nzalo yami isala kutshelwa sibona ngomopho,
Impela sumpophoma igazi ubusuku nemini,
Ukube wangilalela nzalo wayofunda,
Khiwane lami ukube awulibalwanga zibozi nezibungu zimosha ikusasa lakho ngabe...
Awu zibulo nothunjana wami ngabe ngiyaziqhenya ngawe,
Kodwa namhlanje ngidinda esikaNandi, Ikhiwane ziliqedile izibozi
Ikhiwane elihle lidliwa zibozi.

XOLISILE MBALI MABASO

The Beautiful Fig

My hope my daughter my beautiful fig,
Who has green leaves winter and summer. My heroine I was proud of you,
Truly I never thought myself crying over being disappointed by you
In you I saw a nursing sister
The light of this home today, look has turned into nothing,
I thought when I advised you my child you were listening
How intelligent you were my child I thought you would be someone in the future.
But today, my child, I cannot take pride in you, you don't even look like you are educated my first-born child.
If you listened to my advice and lived according to my words you would be in greener pastures,
I know my child, mistakes happen, but from you I expected better because you were informed.
Today you are gravely ill, your failure to heed advice have cost you,
My child those who do not want to be advised are doomed to perdition,
Indeed you have known the fall of blood day in and day out
If you listened to my advice and concentrated on education,
My beautiful fig if only you did not waste your time with decay and worms wasting your future you would have…
Indeed my only child if you listened to me I would have been proud of you,

But today I cry like Zulus after the death of Nandi, worms have finished my fig
A beautiful fig is eaten by worms

Translated from the Zulu original – Ikhiwane Elihle – *by Innocentia Mhlambi*

Esicongweni
Zulu

Usuku lwanamuhla luyinkosi yazo zonke ezinye izinsuku.
Ezinhle nezimbi ziyobuswa yilo lolu.
Ezibuhlungu nezimnandi zizohlonipha lona.
Namuhla ngisesicongweni.

Ukhalo olude lube nzima.
Izinyembezi zami zokuqala zaziwuphawu losizi.
Eyami impilo yaqala mina ngiwumthwalo.
Ngiyabonga namuhla angisiwo umthwalo owehlule.
Nabazali bami bayasho ukuthi umthwalo ngibethule.
Nabakwethu abasakhali bathule.

Namuhla ngisesicongweni.
Ngelula isandla ngithinte isibhakabhaka
Bese kwehla imvula yentokozo.
Ngimoyizelelwa nayilanga imbala.
Ngishawa umoya omnandi
Opholisa igazi lami ngemuva kokusebenza kanzima ngokuzikhandla.
Amehlo ami asebheka abone kude.
Asebukhali kanti nomhlaba usucace bha.
Noma ungahlaba mina sengiwuhlomele ngiwugqokele.
Naphezu kwemvunulo yami ngiwugqokele ijazi elimnyama ngiyayikizela.
Sengethweswe imiyezane.

Inhliziyo yami igcwele intobeko.
Kukude lapho engibuya khona

Kodwa kukude kakhulu lapho engisayakhona
Ngoba manje ngisesicongweni.

Esicongweni kusekhaya lamaqhawe
Amanye awo aphulukundlele sebevale ngemithetho
yobandlululo ontamolukhuni.
Abanye baphume emakhaya bempunga ikati lilele eziko.
Bonke babuye sebechachambile nekati lakubo lathola owalo
umbhede othokomele.

Esicongweni nobengebani uyahlonishwa.
Nobengenazwi usenelungelo lokulalelwa.
Emagunjini ezikhulu ukhulumisa akufunde enyuvesi
izinombolo zivune yena.
Nekhaya lakhe aliphendule libe yisidleke esefudumele
Kufudumale nekusasa.

Esicongweni kukwandlala kayihlali.
Ngoba ixoshwa yijazi, imiyezane neziqu.
Zona zikhuluma kube kanye
Okushiwo yizo kuyiqiniso elamukeleka kahle.
Elazo izwi liqopha umlando wona usekele isizwe.
Kwethabe izinhliziyo kuthinteke namanoni.
Wozani esicongweni…

GIVEN SIBUSISO MAJOLA

At the Pinnacle

Today is the king of all the days.
The good and the bad will be ruled by this one.
The painful and happy ones will respect this one.
Today I am at the peak.

The longest road was difficult.
My initial tears were of sorrow.
My life started off when I was a burden.
I am grateful today I am not a burden that failed
Even my parents are grateful that I have taken off the burden
Even my family is no longer crying silently.

Today I am at the peak.
I stretch out my hand and touch the sky.
And the rain of joy comes down.
Even the sun smiles at me.
I am caressed by the breeze.
That cools the blood after working hard
My eyes are cast far away
They see clearly and the world is crystal clear.
Even if the earth can prickle me I am now fully armed.
Even on top of my traditional clothes I am also dressed in a gown, robes and hoods.
I have been conferred with a degree.

My heart is overfilled with humility.
I come from very far.
But it is still even very far where I am going.
Because now I am at the pinnacle.

The pinnacle is the home of heroes.
Some broke through even when the racist barred them with laws.
Others left their home cats sleeping near the heath.
They all came back alive even their home cats found a warm place to sleep.

At the pinnacle even the non-connected are respected.
Even the voiceless has a right to be heard.
In high offices they talk to what they read at university and the numbers agree with them.
Even their home is turned into a warm nest.
Even the future gets to be warm.

At the pinnacle poverty has no space.
Because it is chased by degrees and robes.
They talk just once.
What they say is the well accepted truth.
Their voice record history which is the foundation of the nation.
At the hearts are gladdened and the spirit is contented.
Come to the pinnacle…

Translated from the Zulu original – Esicongweni – *by Innocentia Mhlambi*

Ke sa gopola
Sepedi

Ke sa mmona le bjale
Mogopolong wa ka o sa ralala
Mola tša gagwe diatla ke sa dikwa di tematemiša wa ka mmele
Mahlo a gagwe a gore hubee boka madi
Ke sa bona a ntebeletše ka tlhologelo le tšhošetšo,
Fahlego sa gagwe sa go tšhutšhuthela boka sa bata sa lešoka
Le ge ke pontše mahlo ke sa se bona
Melongwana ya gagwe ya go omelela ka tlala le nyora la legogwa
Ke sa ekwa e sepelasepela godimo ga ya ka
Le ge tswalo la ka le be le betha wa go rutlulla tlhaka ya ngwako
Maotwana'ka o ka rego a letlorontlope
A mananana, a se nkego a phopholwa ke pholo
Ga se nka a ba pelopedi go a phatlalatša bjalo ka kgorwana di sego tša notlelwa
Go ya ka kgopolo go sa duma koša yeo a bego a nkopelela ge a be a hlagatša legogwa
A itsholetše ka mogopo ' bile melomo e rotharotha ditete ka boipshino
O be a realo; ge nka re poo, gagešo ke thabeng!
Sellwana sa ka sa go se sekegelwe tsebe, e be e ke se mo tšhela makhura
Masetlapelo, ka re ke le mothepa, ka pšhatlwa ditlolamelora ke serolorolo sa mabadi
Phaga' go ikgela merogo tšhemong tše nanana.
Sethokgwa se lego go wa gagwe mmele, go tšwela ntle se a mpoifiša,

Mmalo! Setseketseke sa tla sa ntshenyetša bophelo
Tlhaologanyong ke bodile ke sa nkga mekgatho
Ka mare ke itshwela etšwe phošo e se ya ka
Bangwe ba nkodutla, ba segiša ka nna
Bophelo ga ke sa bona, ke ra bokamoso
Moya o a tšokatšoka,
A ntirilego ke di bona bošego le mosegare
Le muši ya dikwekwele e ile tshepo,
Ka wa seloko monga khutšo e subeletše,
Ke tla ratwa ke mang ge ke itlhoile?
Go ikamogela ke thaba,
Motho yola go wa ka mmele o ikgašitše
Tsebe mpheng le ntlhakodiše,
Ke fenywa ke bohloko.

                              T<small>SHEPISO</small> M<small>AKGOLOANE</small>

I Remember

I still see him
He still dominates my mind
His hands I still feel touching my body
His red bloodshot eyes
Staring at me with a yearning and intimidation,
His flaming face scary like a wild beast
Even with my eyes closed
His lips parched by hunger and sexual lust
I can still feel them forced on mine
Though my heartbeat threatened to tear the roof off
My skinny feet
Soft and not yet touched by a man
He never thought twice before parting them like an unlocked door
I can still hear the song he sang as he tore into me
As he served himself his mouth dripping with enjoyment
He said if I made any noise he'll kill me!
My muffled cry was like fuel to his violence
The bigger tragedy is to be ravaged by an old man while I am still a young girl
They violate them young and tender
I'm intimidated by the forest in his body,
Oh My God! A loser destroyed my life
Traumatised me while still young
I blame myself while I am not the guilty one
Some spite and laugh at me
Life is worthless, tomorrow is dim
My soul is tormented
I relive the trauma every minute of the day

I'm hopeless
Restless
Who will love a person who can't self-love?
It's difficult to accept
He planted himself in my body
Listen to me and save me
My pain threatens to defeat me

Translated from the Sepedi original – Ke sa gopola – *by Goodenough Mashego*

O fetotše!
Sepedi

Ba go go tseba ba re o monolofatši,
Bangwe ba re o mothatafiši.
O fihlile lefaseng la borakgolokhukhu wa fetola,
Ditsebja ke wena wa se kgaotše go di hlola.

O hweditše go lengwa ka diatla le makaba,
Wa hlola diterekere, wa ba tlaba.
O hweditše go sepelwa ka dinao,
Wa hlola ditimela, gwa khutšišwa dinao.

Wa fetola tšohle,
Gwa šomišwa wena gohle.
Mešomo yohle ya dirwa ke wena,
Ga go se na le mešomo, e tšerwe ke wena.

Bo rakgolokhukhu ga ba sa šoma,
Dipolaseng o tsene, bo tate ga ba sa šoma.
Mabele o a buna, diaparo o a roka.
Mabele o a šila, tšohle re a reka.

Tlala e wele ga re na bahomotši,
O tlile le bobodu, o hlotše le malwetši.
O rile o tlo dira dilo bonolo,
Kganthe o tlo hlola ditsikitlano tša meno le boitsholo.

O hlotše dilo go thwe ke diselula,
Ga di tšwafe go gorošoša ya maka melaetša.
Re bolela le ba mošwa mawatle re filo dula,
Le go lwiša di a kgona, mekutwana di a phušulla.

                              CHARLES JULIE MAKOFANE

You responded!

Those who know you say you are simplifier,
Other say you make things difficult.
You arrived at the world of our ancestors and responded,
Didn't stop creating that which you know

They farmed with hands and cattle,
You puzzled them by inventing tractors.
Your found them walking
Rested their feet by inventing trains.

You changed everything
Became a household item
Performed all jobs and chores
You took all the jobs

Our grandparents no longer work
You are in farms, our fathers are unemployed
You harvest corn, and make clothes
You grind mielies, we buy everything

Hunger is everywhere we have no comforters
You brought laziness, invented disease
You said you'll make things simpler
All you brought is the gnashing of teeth and regret

You invented things called cellular phones
They never fail to deliver fake news
They connect us
They often incite conflict and destroy families

Translated from the Sepedi original – O fetotše! – *by Goodenough Mashego*

Diaila o kae?
Sepedi

Mola nkabe bahu ba tsoga,
Nkabe ba tlo niša pula ya matlorotloro.
Lefaseng ke dipshišamare, o ka betologa
Diaila o ile, lefaseng go šoro!

Bahlologadi ba thwathwaša la phukubje,
Mola bahlolo ba hlabelwa ke letšatši phogong.
Bana ba apešana mapai le bakgalabje.
Ruri Diaila o ile, o re šile tlalelong.

Bana ba belega bana,
Banna ba kga merogo barweding.
Ga go sa na yo mogolo, ga go sa na ngwana
Diaila o hwile, ga go sa na melao ka malapeng.

Diaila o kae?
O re šile pepeneneng, matlorotlorong!
Lefaseng go senyegile, re tšhabele kae?
Ruri o re lahlile, hle tla o re nyorolle leganateng!

CHARLES JULIE MAKOFANE

Where are bad omens?

If the dead could be resurrected,
They would bring down a torrent
The world is a disgrace
No more bad omens, the world is vile!

Widows howl like jackals
While widowers are found wanting
Babies share beds with old men
No more bad omens, we are left frustrated

Babies give birth to babies
Fathers commit incest with daughters
Age has become nothing but a number
Bad omens are dead, there's no order in households

Where are you bad omen?
You left us exposed, in a torrent!
The world is disgraceful, where shall we flee?
You abandoned us, please come quench our thirst!

Translated from the Sepedi original – Diaila o kae? – *by Goodenough Mashego*

Kungusizi
Zulu

Kungusizi konke lokhu okuhlezi lapha
Kuyabala, kuqhathanise osekwasala
Kubuyisela emuva isikhathi, kwehluleke bese kuyakhala
Kuyaziqhathulula, kuphike okuyikho kubike izaba
Pho-ke inhliziyo kayiphakelwa, konke yimbala
Nokho kungusizi konke lokhu okuhlezi lapha.

Kuzungeza ndawonye
Qede kukhalaze ngebanga
Kulalela phimbo linye
Qede kubalise ngokuthi bonke bayefana
Kuhlala phansi kwethunzi
Qede kukhale ngokungabibikho kwelanga
Kuzigwaza kona qede kukhombe omunye ngesandla
Wo! kungusizi konke lokhu okuhlezi lapha.

Kuzihayela kona izinkondlo, kushayele abanye ihlombe
Kuhuba ubuhle, bubunamathisele kwabanye
Uthi kuyazibona ukufaneleka kukho?
Cha-bo, kungusizi konke lokhu okuhlezi lapha.

MBALI MALIMELA

It is sorrow

It is sorrow all that is seated here
It is counting, and compared that which remains
It takes back time, fails and then it cries
It causes its own fall, deny what is there and make excuses
But then one never dishes for the heart, all is reality
Nonetheless it is sorrow all that is seated here

It goes round in circles
Thereafter complains about the distance
It listens to one voice
Then complain that all are the same
It sits under the shadow
Then complains about the lack of sun
It stabs itself then with another hand points at the other
Wo! It is sorrow all that is seated here

It sings poetry to itself, and clap for others
It sings beauty, and paste it to others
Do you think it sees its suitability?
No, it is sorrow all that is seated here.

Translated from the Zulu original – **Kungusizi** – *by Innocentia Mlhambi*

Isandla
Xhosa

Sakha ngononophelo nangobuchule
Kodwa sibuye sitshabalalise ngephanyazo
Singumbumbi wokuhle
Sikwangumtshabalalisi wokuhle
Sihlala singcangcazela singcungcutheka kukubon'okuhle

Kuthi kubuya zingcinga zimbi sibe sesiququmbele
Sihlala sifumbethe inzondo, imithambo yaso ibaleka urhwaphilizo, nokuxhaphaza, nokoxutha isidima samanina
Sona siyakuxhawula sikushiye uxhelekile emphefumlweni nase nyameni

Makwehle esakho Lang'lokulunga kuba kaloku esakho asisifitshane ukuba singesindisi
Esakho sibuye sibene mfesane kodwa esomvuziselo wakho simasikisizi, kuyoyikeka ukuwela kuso
Sidyobheke ezonweni, sihlel'elishweni!

NANGAMSO MALU

The Hand

The hand builds with care and skill
But it can destroy with suddenness
It is the moulder of beauty
It can also be the destroyer of beauty
It always trembles when it sees beauty
By the time stray thoughts come along it has already finished

It always possesses hatred, in its veins runs corruption, abusiveness, and taking away the dignity of women
It will shake your hand and leave you devastated in your spirit and body,

Let yours descend upon us Sun of righteousness, because yours is not short, and would not save us
Yours is compassionate but your rewarding is disgusting, it is scary falling into it,
It is drowning in sins, it remains in bad luck.

Translated from the Zulu original – **Isandla** – *by Innocentia Mlhambi*

Home
for Gus Thompson

You no longer knew your name, nor where you lived, nor
the peak you loved to hike that rises from the waves, that dome of
granite, gusts and foam, where you once dreamed your ashes would be freed
And yet, some deeper call urged you to flee the safe place of walls and lights
and walk straight there, surefooted through the night, arms swinging
as though some primal song knew all along where you belonged
the way the swallow knows true north, and listens to its longing
winging its way home, the way the river finds the sea

There followed six long days of searching
and sniffer dogs and drones, desperation
gnawing to the bone, and swallowed hope
more hollow with each sunset, till
they found your body where you left it, still
seated in the morning sun at rest beside a river,
no struggle on your face as you looked out
from your chosen place to sea, simply peace
released from the crosswires of your nameless worlds
into the last dark fire of daybreak

SUSAN CLARE MANN

Tshomo
Sesotho

Ba re e ne e re; Qooi!

Ke hopola ha ke ne ke le monyenyane,
E le nna le nna, ausi-kgaetsedi le nna,
Bosiu bo fafatsa serame,
Bo jetse peo tse kganyang lefifing,
Mme lehae la mollo le tuka ho futhumatsa,
Ausi-kgaetsedi a tshwela taba tsa kgale,
A di pepeta sa boMmadiatheng,
Taba tsa leleme la Sesotho, tsa bo nkgono ho tswa ho feta:
Nanana Boselesele; Tselane le Dimo.

Mantswe e le ditshwantsho tsa ho ikgantsha,
Nako e phalla sa noka,
E le nna le nna, ausi-kgaetsedi le nna,
Ha se le itse pote, ngwanabo mosweu a se a ipopile,
A re; "Pere ya mme, pere ya mme tlo ke kgutse,
Pere ya mme, pere ya mme tlo ke kgutse,
Ke nna Manko, ke nna Hmm,
Ke nna Manko, ke nna Hmm."

A di qhebolla ka mefuta tsebeng tsa ka,
Ho fihlela boroko bo nka bo be bo re;
"Ya ba ke tshomo ka matheto!"

NORMAN MARAPO

Mystery

They say it said, Qooi!

I remember when I was young
Me and myself, my sister and I
The night was cold
Having planted shiny seeds in the dark
Home is where the heart is
My sister narrating old tales
Telling them like Mmadiatheng
Stories about Sesotho language, of grandmothers and beyond:
Nanana Boselesele; Tselane and Dimo

Words like proud pictures
Time flows like a river
Me and myself, my sister and I
After the sun has set and she has composed herself
She would say, "Mother's horse, mother's horse let me pause,
Mother's horse, mother's horse let me pause
I am Manko, I am Hmm
I am Manko, I am Hmm"

In my ears all types were destroyed
Until sleep took over and said;
"And it is a mystery"

Translated from the Sesotho original – Tshomo – by Goodenough Mashego

Pad
(Na die beeldhouwerk Path *deur Florian Wozniak)*
Afrikaans

'n Man waad deur 'n grasland.

  'n Man waad deur 'n grasland en sy hand
   vaar   oor die grasaar

  sy hand bid   'n versigtige bevoeling van kosbaarheid
  'n teer beluistering vir   die vlinders van 'n polsslag
     roerend tussen die stingels
  die gras wat heuphoogte
       om hom vou en sluit, vou en sluit

'n Man waad deur 'n grasland
   en dit word een lang glissando   Braille vir 'n dowe
met note waarna hy nooit weer terug sal keer nie

'n Man waad deur 'n grasland
   miskien desperaat, miskien net op pad
                   die grashalms domino

'n Man waad deur 'n grasland en die ganse grasland
                word sy gewaad

                           MARIETA MCGRATH

Path
(Inspired by the Path *sculpture by Florian Wozniak)*

A man wades through grassland.
  A man wades through grassland and his hand
  sails across the ears of grass

  his hand prays   careful caresses wealth
  listens tenderly for   the fluttering of a pulse
      stirring between stalks
  the grass high as his hips
      opens and closes around him, opens and closes

A man wades through grassland
  everything becomes one long glissando   braille for a deaf person
  notes he will never return to

A man wades through grassland
  perhaps he's desperate, perhaps he's just on his way
                              the ears of grass
domino

A man wades through grassland and the whole veld
                                becomes his garment

Translated from the Afrikaans original – Pad *– by Pieter Odendaal*

Off-grid
Afrikaans

Laataand, breinloos, blaai ons
deur algoritmiese voorstelle
op YouTube.

Nog 'n man (en sy vrou en sy hond)
wat nie meer maklik wou leef nie.
Sy lewe was te vanselfsprekend;
een aand het hy sy hande geklap
vir die staanlamp langs die bank,
die kilhelder lig moeiteloos ontvang

en hy was gebaai in die skuld.

"Daarom is ek hier, kniediep in die sneeu
voor my handgemaakte huis van hout."

Sy donsbaadjie rafel om die moue
(is dit Made in China? wonder ek)
en hy lap dit met stukkies plastiek
voor hy sy slee volpak met
die modernste visvanggerei.

Om te eet, moes hy leer visvang.

Voor hy deur die ys boor, plaas hy eers sy kamera:
'n swart stippel op 'n eindelose kraakwit wildernis,
hyself op 'n safarigroen stoel,
wat wag op sy visstokke
om verdag te roer.

'n Man van min woorde,
laat hy sy hond die praatwerk doen:
"Kyk hoe hy uitbundig sneeu
met sy blinkswart snoet verstrooi!"
(Maar ek ken honde, hulle sal selfs op die Noordpool
gelukkig wees.)

Laataand klap die man sy skootrekenaar oop.
Hy moet vandag se video's sny
en op die wêreldwye web laai.
Dis 'n vanselfsprekende stroom van inkomste
as mense soos ek breinloos
laatnag daarop klik.

Marieta McGrath

Off-grid

Late at night, braindead, we page
through algorithmic suggestions
on YouTube.

Yet another man (and his wife and his dog)
who no longer wanted an easy life.
His life was too obvious;
one night he clapped his hands
for the pedestal lamp next to the sofa,
effortlessly welcoming the icy light

and he was bathed in guilt.

"That's why I'm here, knee-deep in the snow
in front of my hand-built house of wood."

His fleece jacket is frayed around the sleeves
(is it Made in China? I wonder)
he mends it with patches of plastic
before he fills his sled
with state-of-the-art fishing gear.

He had to learn to fish to eat.

Before drilling through the ice, he sets up his camera:
a black spot in the endless gleaming-white wilderness,
he sits on a safari-green chair,
waits for his fishing rods
to stir suspiciously.

A man of few words,
he lets his dog do the talking:
"Look at him exuberantly scattering
snow with his wet, black snout."
(But I know dogs, they'll always be happy,
even at the North Pole.)

Later that evening the man flips his laptop open.
He must edit today's footage
and upload it to the worldwide web.
It's a self-evident stream of income
when braindead people like me
click on his videos late at night.

Translated from the Afrikaans original – **Off-grid** – *by Pieter Odendaal*

Burnt Orange

burnt orange
a tinge blended
in the gut; hued
& hewed
from the pith of the core

the lava
of my depths
the intensities of smile, pang & doubling over
the fingers, hand, arm in dog-leg splint
reaching back through time

through times
churning, fertile
wild, yeasting, effervescent
from latent pause to crackling
and simmering light from the blistered sun

burnt child
burnt world
singed moon

burnt orange, the moments, those fragments
my Khoiness; by day, shimmering under boundless sky
at night, with scorched edges
    and under the deep violet
    the burnt orange, hard baked

from worlds before
 toasted orange
peppered with
craps of bark, crushed dry leaf, trace elements from river shale
… ochre in the gut of these words

FRANK MEINTJIES

Ubhubhane weKhovithi
Xhosa

Satshayel' isitshingitshane lingekatshon' ilanga,
Satshayela okomtshayelo omtsha kraca.
Yatshayel' itshambaz' intsholongwane,
Itshil' itsheleza okwentshili itshayelela,
Itsholoz' itshotsholoz' okwenkwenkw' omtshotsho,
Itshent' itshabalalis' omdala nomtsha.

Yaqhwitsha qhitshwi okomatshisi!
Itshis' ingatshabalalisi matshitshi namatshijol' odwa.
Yayitshabalalis' imitshato isemitsha,
Basala bematshekil' abatshakazana ngeekhetshemiya.
Latshetshisa lalal' umbeth' itshoba komdala nakomtsha,
Lasal' ilizwe limbatshile, litshazile.

Satshitshiliza sitshutshiswa ngumtshutshisi,
Ekhatshwa zizililo kuyintsholo.
Batshilo bathi yintsholongwan' aseTshayina,
Ukhetsh' otshayel' isikhukukazi namantshontsho.

Tyhini! Kumhla ndalufun' ugonyo, ndalangazelel' ivaksini.
Andakhathelela nabo bandiwa ngentsi-i-ini!

PHINDILE MEMANI

Covid Pandemic

A tornado swept before sun set,
It swept like a brand new broom,
The virus swept indiscriminately,
It burned everything like the velt fire, making sure it burns everything in its way
It was dancing going forward like a boy at a reed dance,
Destroying the young and the old

It sparked like the lighting of matches
It destroyed everyone including the virgins and those with experience
It destroyed new marriages,
The brides were left wandering in their cashmeres
Quickly, both the young and old died,
The country was left in despair

We were being prosecuted by the prosecutor
Accompanied by cries everywhere
They said that it was the virus from China
A hawk that sweeps over the hen and its chicks

Alas! How I longed for a vaccine
I did not care about those who were laughing at me!

Translated from the Xhosa original – Ubhubhane weKhovithi
– *by Innocentia Mhlambi*

Dlal'uhadi
Xhosa

Ekugqibeleni!
Nam ndidendathweswa ingubo yemfundo,
Ndajika ndasisifundiswa esizalwa liqabakazi.
Ingathi nguthikra kulamagx'atsolo,
Inene ndifana nehomba madoda.
Dlal'uhadi nozala wen'ozel'isifundiswa.

Ekugqibeleni!
Ndiyiqhawulile imigibo ndatsiba neendonga,
Ndiyiwelile imifula, ndaziqabela neentaba,
Ndigxadazel'emigxobhozweni ndixhinishela,
Ndidyobhadyobheka ndintyumpantyumpeka ezihogweni.
Hayi! Dlal'uhadi nozala wen'ozel'isifundiswa.

Imimoya nezaqwithi zindibhubhudlile,
Imvula nenkungu zindinethile.
Amaqhwa neqabaka zindiqhaqhathekisile,
Ukanti imibethe yona ndiyibhula ngezikatshiwo,
Ndisinge esikolweni nakumaziko emfundo.
Dlal'uhadi nozala wen'ozel'isifundiswa.

Ndiqhaqhek'ingqondo ndaqonda ngqo,
Ndityebile lulwazi ndondlisisiwe,
Ndikatsiwe kwaye ndikatsekile.
Hayi! Dlal'uhadi nozala wen'ozel'isifundiswa.

Dlal'uhadi ugcobel'isithwalandwe,
Dlal'uhadi ungalibal'ukuthandaz'ubulel'uThixo.
Dlal'uhadi ubike nakumanyange nezinyanya,
Dlal'uhadi nozala wen'ozel'isifundiswa.

TLOTLISANG DAVID MHLAMBISO

Play the Harp

At last!
I have received the garment of education
I became an educated person born by an illiterate woman
I stand out on these sharp should
Indeed I am a neat person
Play the harp mother you who has birthed an educated child

At last
I have destroyed the traps and jumped over the wall
I have crossed rivers and climbed mountains
Navigating through the streams
I have been through the mud and through the rain
Oh! Play the harp you who has birthed an educated child

I have been through strong wind currents
I have been through heavy rains and mist
Snow and ice dew made me shiver
I walked in dew bare footed
Going to school
Play the harp you mother who has birthed an educated child

My mind was dissected and I understood
I have been fed with knowledge
I have been sharpened
Play the harp mother who has birthed an educated child

Play the harp and be happy for the one that wears the gown
Play the harp and don't forget to pray and thank the lord
Play the harp and tell the ancestors
Play the harp you the mother who has given birth to educated child

Translated from the Xhosa original – Dlal'uhadi – *by Innocentia Mhlambi*

Ntinga-Mbhali
Xhosa

Ngendisithi ntinga ntaka,
Kodwa vuma ndithi ntinga mbhali.
Ntinga untingele emafini njengokhozi,
Untingele emajukujukwini esibhakabhaka.

Nting'uziqhenye ngosiba lwakho,
Uxelele isizwe ngokubaluleka kwalo.
Unting'ung'uthi ngcu ezintabeni untyiloze,
Untyiloz'okwentak'ekhrisimesi.

Ugadle mbhali, ugadl'ukhahlele,
Uqabel'eqongeni ubaqokelele
Ubabize bazokusela kumthombo wobomi,
Apho kupholiswa amanxeba obu bomi.

Nting'ubhek'emazwen'aphesheya,
Hlez'ubuye nodumo lwaphesheya.
Zininz'iintshaba kodwa ntinga,
Mininz'imiceli mingeni kodwa ntinga.

Nting'untingele ngasekhaya kaloku,
Usibonis'imisebenzi yakho eyakhayo.
Nting'usiqingel'ikamv'eliqaqambileyo,
Noko amangomso ayathembisa, ntinga.

TLOTLISANG DAVID MHLAMBISO

Fly author

I would say fly bird
But I am saying fly author
Fly to clouds like an eagle
Fly to the horizon of the sky

Fly and be proud about your pen
Tell the nation about its importance
Fly to the mountain tops and chirp
Chirp like bird on Christmas day

Strike them and kick them author
Climb on stage and collect them
Call them to drink in the well of life
Where wounds are healed

Fly to nations abroad
And come back with the fame from abroad
Enemies are plenty but fly
Challenges are but fly

Fly home also
Show us your work
Fly and build us a bright future
At least the future looks promising

Translated from the Xhosa original – **Ntinga-Mbhali** – *by Innocentia Mhlambi*

Akekho ozokulwela
Zulu

Sukuma ulwe
Zabalaza kuze kulunge
Intsha yethu isosizini
Lwezidakamizwa,
Lophuzo oludakayo
Kodwa akekho ozoyilwela

Osopolitiki bayathembisa
Engani bancenge ivoti elizothuthukisa bona
Nemindeni yabo,
Khala kakhulu muntu omusha
Akekho ozokulwela

Thabatha igeja
Buyela ensimini
Izandla zakho mazingavilaphi
Liphuma ilanga lishona, Sukuma

Vula amehlo, landela iziyalo zoyihlo mkhulu
Phindela ensimini.
Ensimini yokuphemba isizwe
Ensimini yokuphemba obaba abaqotho
Ensimini yokwakha omama abaqotho.
Omama bakwaNtu

Uma nilala liyofa elihle kakhulu.
Akekho Ozonilwela

HLENGIWE MNYANDU

There is no one to fight for you

Stand up and fight
Protest until things become alright
Our youth is in the midst of sorrow
Of drugs
Of alcohol
But there is no one to fight for it

Politicians promise
Isn't it that they are begging for a vote that will only advance them
And their families
Cry very hard young person
There is no one to fight for you

Take a hoe
Go back to the fields
Your hands must never be lazy
Day break sun set

Open your eyes, follow the instructions of your ancestors
Go back to the field
The field of kindling a nation
The field of kindling honest fathers
The field of kindling honest mothers
Mothers of KwaNtu

If you sleep this beautiful country will be killed
There is no one to fight for you.

Translated from the Zulu original – Akekho ozokulwela – *by Innocentia Mhlambi*

Mina bengithi Maluju
Zulu

Ngizwe isililo
Phakathi kwamabili
Ngezwa isililo
Entathakusa
Izwi lowesifazane
Likhala kalusizi
Lithi yini icala
Lami na?
Kodwa
Izimpendulo azitholakalanga
Kepha igazi lowesifazane
Laphalala kabuhlungu
Ebalisa, exolisa
Encenga, ecela ithuba
Lesibili empilweni
Kodwa isandla esinonya
Asimlalelanga
Mina bengithi Maluju!!!

Ngibone umama ethwele
Izandla ekhanda elila
Kalusizi
Ethi umntanami wenzeni na?
Yelekelelani bo!!!
Kodwa isandla esinonya
Asimlalelanga
Mina bengithi Maluju!!!

Umntwanyana
Omncanyana
Obefisa ukukhula
Abe nekusasa
Eliqhakaqizile
Obeyithemba
Labazali bakhe
Isandla esinonya
Simshabalalisile
Aphela onke
Amathemba
Mina bengithi Maluju!!!

Kanti lenzondo engaka
Ngeyani na
Wenzeni owesifazane
Ongenamandla ?
Okuzivikela na?
Yibo na yini ubuqhawe?
Lobo na?
Ake uzifune uzithole
Sandla sembubhiso
Mina bengithi Maluju!!!

CHARITY BAKHAKAMILE MNYANDU

I am calling for truce

I heard anguished screaming
In the middle of the night
I heard anguished cries
Towards dawn
It is the voice of a woman
Sorrowfully crying
It asked what is the charge
What am I guilty of?
But
The answers were not found
But the blood of the woman
Is spilt very harrowingly
Trying to explain, asking for forgiveness
Begging, asking for a chance
A second in life
But the evil hand
Did not listen to her
I am asking for truce!!!

I saw a woman carrying
Her hands on her head crying
In sorrow
Asking what wrong did my child do?
Please help!!!
But the evil hand
Did not listen to her
I am asking for truce

A child
Very little
Who wished to grow up
And have a future
That is bright
Who was the hope
Of their parents
The evil hand
Disappeared them
Finished
Are all hopes
I am asking for truce

But this hatred
What is it for
What is the woman guilty of?
Who is powerless?
To protect herself?
Is this your idea of heroism?
Is that it?
You must introspect and find yourself
Hand of destruction
I am asking for truce!!!

Translated from the Zulu original – Mina bengithi Maluju – *by Innocentia Mhlambi*

Moswa ke a lla
Sepedi

Kgakanego o nkapere boka Kgomara
Dithokgwa di omile le phuthi ga e tšwe
Ke rutegile ka tshepa dibana sa pele
La dithuto le aperwe ke leboto
Ke gatile bolele ka pharagana

Baswana le boletše la re golang le di bone
A ka mathata ke moswananoši
Setšo ke lahlile marata helele ka latela tša batho
Ke tla kokota go diputswa di nkgakolle
Le fahlilwe le lebeletše

Ke a thiba go a dutla
Ke a aga go a thoboga
Dikgaphampsikela di kgelempuwa ka nna
Mahlajana a feletše lefeeleng
Ke kgotsa ke sa fetše

Ke tlhokatsebe senyatša batswadi
Ke kopane natšo di a ntlaba
Ke nyatša molala ke hwela nyanyeng
Ke segwa ke tša go fofa lefaufaung
Ke rile ke tšhipu mohlaba o ntlabile

Ke kgapha malwetšisetsebje se šita bašweu
Tšhiwana di ntšhupa thopeng ya rakgolo
Dipheko ke swaswitše ka ipha borwa

Bjale le go kodimela ke a šitwa
Ke gopotše le muši wa dišu
Naga ka efa bafihlani
Ba ntšhela phorimahlong ka lesome
Temo e nthona sejalešela
Dirafša tša tšewa ka mebalabala
Bjale le ya le letala ga ke nayo

Bogoši ke bo fularetše dikokwane di le gona
Tšhabana sa tate se phatlaletše
Re bušwa ke bommakaipea bogoši ke a latola
Ga ke fetele ke se lekhwekhwe
Le wa mphatong ga ba ntsebe

Ke ngwana llela nakana mokhura
Legano le a ntlaba le bodila
Ke beile molomo ka bogola boka mpša
Ke tshetše noka go bowa go a pala
Moswa ke a lla

Ke jele sethiba molomo
Ka ya ntlo leswiswi le dithaka
Ka boa tša re leswiswi
Lenyatšo la ntheoša le noka Tubatse
Le go gola tšie go a pala

Ke goma ka megolo ke mokgakgati
Ngwana phoša dira hle
Segagabo motho se a ntšhita
A bagologolo le kwa leleme lešele?
A gona tsela ke tla bulelwa ke mang?

MMABORE GLADYS MOGASHOA

A youth's lament

Confusion wears me like a second skin
The future looks uncertain little is moving
I got education put my trust in books
My degree hangs on the wall
I stepped on algae slipped and fell

Our forebears you warned us with age comes experience
My problems are unique
My culture I abandoned and followed other nations
I'll seek guidance from my elders
I saw it coming

Nothing I do manifests
Everything I build collapses
Giants use me as a a stepping stone
My wisdom has faded
I am forever astounded

I'm hard-headed I disrespect parents
I'm puzzled by what I see today
"Fool me twice shame on me"
Even birds laugh at me
I'm learning my lessons the hard way

I spread alien diseases that defeat western medicine
Orphans point me to my grandfather's secret
I mocked my heritage and strayed

Today I can't even persevere
I miss smoke from waste

I gave the land to arrivals
They bribed me with money
Farming not for me snazzy dresser
Minerals are confiscated in different colours
Now I don't even have bare minimums

I turned my back on my kingship while pillars I had
My father's tribe is scattered
We are ruled by self-appointed I wash my hands on kingship
I don't infect while not being rash
At the royal kraal they know me not

I'm the child who was given all he wanted
My mouth is bitter
Through my mouth I barked like a dog
I crossed the river and can't return
Youth I'm crying

In a face mask
I went to jail with my peers
Returned to darkness
Disrespect sent me down Tubatse river
I can't even fend for myself

My pain is self-inflicted
First-time offender
I know nothing of my culture
Do my ancestors hear a foreign language?
Who will pave the way for me?

Translated from the Sepedi original – Moswa ke a lla – *by Goodenough Mashego*

Loso
Setswana

Fokotsa bogale loso,
Ikatle pele le rona re tshege,
Ema pele le rona re itumele,
Tsatsi le letsatsi ke dikeledi.
Go lekane fokotsa bogale.

Senokwane; fokotsa go re utswetsa,
O selo mang o mekamekana le Maikutlo a rona?
Ka nnete o ngwetsi ya malapa otlhe,
Re utlwele botlhoko o tlogele tiro eo.

Bosigo le motshegare, re a boga ke wena,
Kutlobotlhoko malapeng e tlisiswe ke wena, Loso o tswa kae, e bile o boela gae leng?
Loso o rongwa ke mang?
Re utlwile go lekane, wena sera se segolo.
O itse go sulafaletswa batho botshelo.

O noga e lomang e fodisa,
O nta ya selomela kobong,
O magagaru,
Tsa gago thupa mo metsing di ineetswe ke yo o sa bonweng.

REBAONA BOITUMELO REGINAH MORULE

Death

Slow down,
Hold yourself allow us laughter,
Wait let us be happy,
Every day is tears.
It's enough ease your anger.

Crook; stop stealing from us,
What animal are you to mess with our feelings?
You are every family's bride,
Have mercy and spare us the pain

Day and night, we suffer from you
Sadness in families you brought,
When do you return where you come from?
Who sends you?
We have had enough, our greatest foe.
You only know to destroy lives.

You are a snake that bites and heals,
A leech,
A quagmire,
Whoever equipped you to inflict pain is unknown to us.

Translated from the Setswana original – Loso – *by Goodenough Mashego*

Isondo liyajika
Zulu

Uma uphila emafutheni,
Ungatamasi kuze kweqe.
Uma udl' izambane likapondo,
Ungabashalazeli ababhekwa yisambane;
Ungabadeleli abadl' imbuya ngothi.
Um' usakhomba ngophakathi,
Ungahlekisi ngezinkedama.
Impilo yisondo elijikayo,
Kusasa izokususa emsamo,
Ikubeke emnyango.
Ithathe inkedama iyiphendule isicebi.

   CHOICE DIMAKATSO MPANZA

The wheel turns

When your life is in the lap of luxury,
Don't enjoy excessively
When you are rich,
Don't ignore the poor;
Don't look down on the poverty stricken.
If you are living large
Don't make fun of the poor.
Life is a wheel that turns,
Tomorrow it takes you from the rear,
And places you in front.
And take the poor and make them rich.

Translated from the Zulu original – **Isondo liyajika** – *by Innocentia Mhlambi*

Umlayezo kwaba shonelwe
Zulu

Ngidinga uk'khuluma naba shonelwe
Ngidinga uk'khuluma naba sanda ukshonelwa
Labhe khona ngiya kholwa bhasengakakholwa
Kubi ingathi kungavela noma mhlabe
uDokotela evese ethi
'Ngiyaxolisa Senze iphutha akyena Oshonile"
Ingobha ngiya khumbula nami lelo langa lobho b'suku bethi
akasekho,kwakuthi agbuze ukuthi
"akasekho" useshonephi
Ningalinge nithi akasekho usesishiyile emhlabeni"
angiyo phinde ngimbone,
angiyo phinde ngizwe izwi lakhe,
kanye nampatho yakhe engangiyiqcina ngalelo Langa
Ngidinga uk'khuluma naba shonelwe…
Mihla nama langa nganginethemba ngizophinde ngimbone
Labhem' fihle khona, la ayifihle khona emhlabeni
Kwase k'fika uma esethi
"mdedele, myekele elale ngoxolo
ngoba ngokwenyama akasekho
kodwa ngoko moya usakhona
Ukumlangazelela kwami ngaka akuyomnika uk'thula la ekhona

SIMPHIWE MTHOMBENI

A message to the bereaved

I need to speak to the bereaved
I need to speak to those recently bereaved
Wherever they are, they have not believed
It is bad, it is as though maybe
a Doctor will just say
"I am sorry we made a mistake, it is not them that died"
It is because I also remember that night when they said to me
They are no longer with us, it was as if I could ask
They are no longer with us, where did go
Don't ever say he is no longer with us, he has left us in this earth
I am never to see them again
I will never hear their voice again
and also their care that I last experienced that Day
I need to talk to those bereaved…
Every day I was hoping I will see them again
Where they have hidden them, where they have hid on this earth
Then it dawned on me
let them go, let them sleep in peace
Because in flesh they are no longer there
But in spirit they are there
My yearning for them this much will not give them rest

Translated from the Zulu original – Umlayezo kwaba shonelwe – *by Innocentia Mhlambi*

Niwafunani amathala?
Xhosa

Niwafunan'amathala?
Lento nihleli nje niyawadililiza!
Niwaphethel'imbengwana niyawabhidliza.
Nide ningalali niwabhulel'amasaka.
Niwakrolonqa iintsimbi niwaphulel'igubasi.
Niwafak'umlilo atsh'abeluthuthu.
Niluhlobo lweziphi na izithuthuthu?
Niqhutywa ngowuphi na babhem ufuthu?

Zange ndaxakwa.
Nithini ngabenu abantwana?
Nithini ngabenu ababhali?
Kudume ukuba asibantu bakhulel'encwadini.

Izenzo zenu zingqinela obobuxoki.
Senide niqinise imixhadi niqhekeza amathala.
Ngumkhwa mni na lo Mzi kaXhosa?
Linyala lantoni na eli Sizwe samaPhara?
Kwamiswa iintshukumo ebantwini.
Suke narhubuluza nishukuma.
Kanti nenza le mbuqe?
Niyavuya ke ngoku x'abantwana bengenalayibhrari?
Niyancuma na xa bekheth'ukuxhwarha ebharini?
Besakubhoreka babimbiliz' intlobo ngentlobo zebhiya
Okwenkom'isel'amanz'emlanjeni.
Anenzen'amathala nihleli nje niyawadiliza?
Abangakhula niyawankula niyawazonda!
Iintsimbi neziseko zawo qho niyazidlikidla.

MADODA NDLAKUSE

Why are you destroying libraries?

Why are destroying libraries?
You are always destroying them
You are forever beating them
You even do not sleep busy beating them
You strip them of their door frames
You burn them down to ashes
What type of fool are you?
What is driving you?

I am bewildered
You say that the children are yours?
What do you say about your authors?
It is said that we are people who do not read

Your actions are supporting these lies
You go to an extent that you break into libraries
What kind of behavior is this?
This nation has become a nation of thieves?
People do not do anything
You are dragging your feet
Only to do this nonsense?
Are you happy now that the children do not have a library?
Do you smile when they choose to go to taverns?
When they are bored they drink all types of beer
Like a cow drinking water in the river
What did libraries do to you as you are always destroying them?

When they grow you are on to them do you hate them!
You destroy all the metals and support structures

Translated from the Xhosa original – Niwafunani amathala? –
by Innocentia Mhlambi

Isoshiyal midiya
Xhosa

Ikukrukra amehlo la ungaboni.
Ikukatsa ubhonge ungaziboni.
Isoshiyal midiya ngogqobhokiley'umdiyadiya.
Ikuhluthel'isidima ngoburhalarhume.
Ikunkala phantsi ubugqwangu bukuvuse.
Ikuhlalela ngezigculelo ikunkule ungenatyala.
Ikuphulukanisa nobunguwe bakho.
Ihleli nje ijong'ithuba lokukujadula.
Ikuqabelisa koy'ekufen' uduladula.
Ikufulela ngemizi yentlungu engqondweni.
Ikukhelel'amanz'ahlwayel'ikhala kwivatala.
Ikugibisel' isiqhalo ngoku sel'ukhala.
Ikurhintyele ngowokuzizonda nokungazixole'umkhala.
Ikubethekisa esithubeni ihambe ikunkala.
Ikukrwinel'ubukrwitsheke sel'uziculela.
Iyakudlalel'uhadi xa ithanda.
Iyakuvulela awonogumbe amathanda.
Ikubonisa lento kuthiwa ngumntu.
Inayo intwana yobuntu.
Iyawavul'evalwa amathuba.
Igcwele ke wethu yimikhuba.
Ingakuxinanisela esi sakho isifuba.
Isakugqiba ikombese izithuko.
Iyakwazi ukuzibaxa izinto.
Igcwel'abanolwaz'oluninzi noxa lungachananga.
Ingakutyhala ukutyhudulela ukuba wenze izigqibo
ezingatshuzanga.

MADODA NDLAKUSE

Social media

It blinds you
It makes you scream without realizing it
Social media is a circus
It brutally takes away your reputation
It throws you down and the ants will pick you up
It makes fun of you and makes you give down judgement
It takes you away from the real you
It is always looking for an opportunity to bring you down
It brings you on to the ride of death
It brings you into a house of mental pain
It will bring you water and drown you in it
It throws you a fruit and you end up crying
It will tie you in the reins of unforgiving self hatred
It will beat you on the head along the way
It will scratch you and you will sing
It will play you the harp when it likes
It will show you good opportunities
It shows you the great side of humanity
It has some humanity
It opens opportunities that are being closed
It is filled with ill-behaved people
It can cause you chest pains
It will overwhelm you with insults on top of that
It knows how to exaggerate things
It is full of people with knowledge though it is not accurate
It can push you to making irrational decisions

Translated from the Xhosa original – Isoshiyal Media – *by Innocentia Mhlambi*

Inyoba ebheka ekufeni
Xhosa

Ibingathi asisagqibi ukubhala,
Sizokwehlukana nekhaya elenz'izigxala,
Sizoodibana nootshomi sihambe sok'dlala.
Sithe sisabuzana malunga noline,
Sabon'inyob'ithrenda saqonda fine.
Sidibanise nje few hundred rands
Saqonda pens down kaloku sana.
Sizakungonwabi ngokuba kutheni thina?
Bayasiqonda phofu ukuba singama2k?
Sikuqhelile ukugroova nokufrika.
Saziwa kuyo yonk'iAfrika.
Singqale ngqo kwaNyobza.
Safik' iibig boys ezinevibe zisilindile.
Yakokotw'ipiano yenz'amaholol'igqom
Sakha salibala ngoMeneer nokukhumbuza ngobudom.
Jonga imali ebikhutshwa phaya!
Ndingaekstenda bonke abanomgogwana bezindlu.
Jonga!bugalelwe eglasini bavele bakhazimla.
Incasa yandibonisa amazwe ndatsho ndibuhlaba.
Ngeengcinga ndakude le phesheya kweZanzibar.
Ndagalela sana andayeka tu Bhabha.
Ndive amehlo am esinda.
Umlomo undongondongo.
Imilebe ibibebezela ingal'ingcangcazela.
Bekukhona ukugxadazela
Iindlebe zisiv'umloz' ongaqhelekanga.
Gqi imfixano kwanqaphel'ukuphefumla.
Ootshomi bam kufutshane nam.
Ndithi bavela bee waca waca.

Okwengca isikwa ngerhenqe.
Ndandiba bayaflora kanti inene.
Ndajikelezelwa bubuchopho.
Intliziyo ingxamil'ukukhangel'umnyango.
Ndive ngesithonga khithatha phantsi zacim'izibane.
Ndavuka emva kweveki sele ndiseMount Frere.
Ndibone ngabantu basekhaya bendirhangqile.
Bandothusa bakundixelel'ukuba sendivel'eFrere.
Bonke bandiqwalasela bengaqhwanyazi
Baza bandibuza umbuzo omnye jwi!
"Mlamli uyakuz' uphinde ubufake emlonyeni"?
Akho wayesazi ukuba andisakwazi ukuthetha
Ndacela usiba nephepha.
Ndavuka ndigxwala ndinjalo kulomandlalo ndabhala.
"Andinakuze ndiyihambe loo nyoba
Kangaka ndingafiki edlakeni ".
Kwathiwa " mfana asinakukugqibela yonke into ikuwe
Izigqibo zakho zonke zixhomekeke kuwe ".

            Madoda Ndlakuse

Happiness that it leading to death

Happiness that is leading to death
It is as if we will not finish writing
We will move away from home that is tiring
We will meet up with friends and we will go and play
We said we are going to ask each other about the line
We saw it trending and thought fine
We gathered few hundred rands
We thought it is pens down
Why should we not make ourselves happy?
They understand that we are 2k's?
We are used to partying
We are known the whole of Africa
We went straight at Nyobza place
We got there the big boys with vibes already waiting
The piano music and gqom music were blasted
Just to forget about the teachers who were reminding us of stupidity
The money that was spent there!
I can build all the small houses
The alcohol was poured in glasses and sparkled
The taste showed me nations and I got into it
In thought I was in Zanzibar
I continued pouring and did not stop
I felt my eyes being heavy
My mouth was numb
My lips were shivering
There was a lot of movement
My ears heard an unfamiliar whistle
Suddenly I could not breath

My friends were near to me
I could see them disappearing
Like grass being cut by a sickle
I thought they were floating
My brain surrounded me
My heart was pacing and looking for a door
I heard a loud sound suddenly I am on the floor
I woke up after a week I was at Mount Frere
I was surrounded by my family
I was shocked when they told me that I was in Frere
The all looked at me without blinking
Then they asked me just one question!
"Mlamli are you going to drink again?"
They knew that I can't no longer speak
I asked for a pen and paper
I woke up in that bed and wrote
"I will no longer participate in that activity
I might not see the end."
They said "My boy we will not make all the decisions for you.
All your decisions depend on you."

Translated from the Xhosa original – Inyoba ebheka ekufeni
– *by Innocentia Mhlambi*

Hamba Nami
Zulu

Nasebumnyameni ukhanya njalo sibani sami.
Yebo, yona indlela iyaphela kepha qhubeka,
Hamba ngethemba nangokukholwa kokuthi
Ukufa kokunye kuwukuzalwa kokunye.
Ungalandeli amaloba abheke ehlane
Hleze akuholele ophathe.

Nanamuhla siphila ngethemba kepha baningi badangele,
Sibambelele kwelithi "kalibulali."
Ngimidwayidwa imivimbo yezinkinga, "kushawa edonsayo."
Iphupho lami ukuthi iphupho lami lifezeke.
Sibani sami khanya njalo nasekukhanyeni,
Usuku umzuzuzwana wokucwayiza,
Busazosifukamela ubumnyama.
Ungangenguli leyongubo yethemba,
Hleze ngiyoxhopheka.

Sithi uyiNkosi yamakhosi, uma sikhuleka.
Eyakho intando yenziwa emaZulwini,
Emhlabeni senza eyethu.
Emagameni amabili elendondana nelikamoya oyingcwele,
UYise kangimazi.
Thando lukababa ngikuzwa ngendaba.
"Lelogqubu lingakuholeli ebumnyameni,
Xola manje nhliziyo,
Phokophela phambili, izolo seledlule,
Ikusasa lakho liqhakazile."
Impela kuyiqiniso ukuthi
Izono zabazali ziwela phezu kwethu, bheka

Sisindwa imithwalo ekungeyona eyethu.

Suka kulelothunzi uphazamisa umoya wami.
Ngilawule moya wami ngilawule,
Hamba nami uyofika ekujuleni lapho
Kukhona ukuthula, intokomalo nentokozo,
Lelochibi lihlanzekile uze ungalidungi.
Hamba nami moya wami, hamba nami.

    ONGEZIWE ONGE NDLANGISA

Accompany Me

Even in the darkness you shine bright my light.
Yes, the road is coming to an end but continue.
Go with the hope and faith that
The death of something else is the resurrection of another thing.
Don't follow others who go to the wilderness.
Perhaps they lead you astray.

Today we live by hope but many are disappointed.
We are holding to a saying that "hope does not kill."
I am scarred by problems, "the forward span is the one that is pushed the hardest."
My dream is for it to come through.
My light shine bright even in the light,
A day is a minute to blink,
Darkness is still to engulf us.
Don't remove from my eyes that blanket of hope,
Perhaps my eyes will be blinded.

We say you are the King of Kings, when we pray.
You will is done in the Heavens,
On earth we do ours.
In the name of two entities the name of the son and of the holy spirit,
Of the Father I do not know.
Love of the father, I don't know you.
"That grudge must not lead you to darkness,
Heart be at peace now,
Look to the future, yesterday is past,

Your future is bright."
Indeed it is the truth that
The sins of the parents fall on us, look
We have been burdened by the load that is not ours.

Remove yourself from that shade you will raise my soul.
Control me my soul, control me,
Accompany me and arrive at the depth where
There is peace, comfort and happiness.
That pool is clean, don't spoil it.
Accompany me my soul, accompany me.

Translated from the Xhosa original – **Hambi Nami** – *by Innocentia Mhlambi*

Nangu uZipho ezivela kuMdali
Zulu

UZipho zemvelo.
Akanakuphucwa.
Akekho emhlabeni ongathi umnikile.
Wafika nazo.
Uhamba nazo.
Uyizo.
Uphila ngazo.
Ziyamuphilisa.
Uphilisa ngazo.
Zinguye.

UZipho zivela kuMdali.
Abametha bengakamboni.
Kodwa uMdali wayesembonile.
UMdali wayesemazile.
Izipho zasezimlindile.
Zasezimazile.

Akazisebenzelanga.
Kepha kuyomele azisebenzise.
Uyazisebenzisa.
Uphila ngazo.
Ziyamuphilisa.
Uphilisa ngazo.
Akekho oyakumphuca.
Azikuzushabalala.

UMdali akazukushabala.
Lapho lezizipho ziqhamuka khona

UMdali umazile ngalezizipho
UMdali umazisile ngalezizipho.
UMdali uzazisile ngalezizipho.

Wazinikeza nobukhulu beziNdlovu.
Azizukuqedeka.
Ziwela ezizukulwaneni.
Ziqhamuka kokhokho.
Ziluleka okwamagatsha.
Ziyakhula.
Gatsheni!
Zihambe zifunwa abantu bebheka Ukuphila.
Ziyaphilisa.
Bayazifuna.
Izipho eziZingelwayo!
Ezingazibeki okwephunga leMpongo!
Izipho eziphilisayo.
Izipho ezivikelayo.
Boya Benyathi!
Ikhaza ulizwa ngendaba.
Izipho zemfudumalo nokukhathalela.
Izipho zothando.
Izipho ezisabekayo.
Ezihloniphekayo.
Ngonyama!
Izipho ezivikelayo.

Izipho ezinyathela kuzamazame umhlaba.
Zipho ezingenasibaya.

Ima khona esicongweni eGatsheni Ndlovu omkhulu.
Wenze okungaziwayo zipho ezinkulu.
Zipho ezingcwele.

Zipho ezivela kuMdali.
Zipho eziveza uMdali.
Zipho ezingaqedekiyo.
Zipho ezinakekelayo.
Eziphilisayo.

Asiphile.
Ndlovukazi yezipho ezivela kuMdali!
Ndlovukazi eyisipho esivela kuMdali.

THALENTE NDLOVU

Here is Zipho's gifts that come from the Creator

UZipho's gifts that are natural.
He cannot be dispossessed.
There is no one on earth who can claim to have bestowed him/her.
S/he was born with them.
S/he will depart with them.
S/he is them.
S/he lives by them.
They give her/him life.
They provide him sustenance.
They are her/him.

UZipho's gifts that come from the Creator.
Who was bestowed a name before they saw her/him.
But the Creator had already seen her/him.
The Creator had already known her/him.
The gifts were already waiting for her/him.
They have already known her/him.

S/he did not work for them.
But it is a must that s/he must use them.
S/he is using them
S/he lives by them.
They give her/him life.
They provide her/him sustenance.
There is no one who can dispossess her/him.
They will never disappear.

The Creator will never disappear.

Where these gifts come from.

The Creator knew her/him by these gifts.
S/he has made the Creator known by these gifts.
The Creator made himself/herself known by these gifts.

He gave them the greatness of the Elephant.
They can never be finished.
They will be transmitted to the next generation.
They come from the ancestors.
They extend like branches.
They grow.
Gatsheni!
They were sought out by people who wanted Life.
They are life giving.
They are wanted.
These are gifts that are Hunted!
That cannot be ignored like the odour of Mpongo!
These gifts are life giving.
The gifts are protective.
Fur of the Buffalo!
The cold you never feel.
The gifts of warmth and caring.
The gifts of love.
The gifts that are fearsome.
That are being respected.
Lion!
The gifts that are protective.

These gifts make steps that cause an earthquake
Gifts without a cattle pen
Stand up at the peak at Gatsheni great Elephant.
Perform the unknown big gifts.
Holy gifts.

Gifts that come from the Creator.
Gifts that manifest the Creator.
Gifts that cannot be finished.
Gifts that protect.
That are life giving.

Let us live.
Elephant of gifts that come from the Creator!
Female Elephant that is a gift from the Creator!

Translated from the Zulu original – Nangu uZipho ezivela kuMdali – *by Innocentia Mhlambi*

Isibindi
Zulu

Umhlaba wami uzungeza inaliti noma igramafoni
Izwi elinzima licula umphefumulo wami phezu
kwe-saxophone
Cha. Linda... Ukushaya kwenhliziyo yami lokho
Uhlobo lwemisindo efana nezintambo zehabhu
Ingoma yempukane eyenza ubusuku buthandane
Isibhakabhaka siphethe izinkanyezi ezingakhanyi
Nezinyanga azishi ngokwanele
Kodwa ebumnyameni ubuso bakhe buyakhazimula
Ngiya phambili, ngimcele umdanso
Elula isandla sami
Nakuba ngingazi ukuthi kufanele nginyathele ngakuphi;
Landela umculo, uzokuyisa lapho
Amazwi kamfowethu, ethukile kodwa, angesabi lutho
Ngizethemba kancane, ngilahlekile kulesi sikhathi
Vala amehlo ami ukuze uqiniseke ukuthi angiphuphi
Ngiphefumula...

LESEGO NKOSI

Courage

My world is going round a needle or a gramaphone
A heavy voice is singing my soul on the gramaphone
No. Wait...Is it that the beating of my heart
It is the type of sounds that are similar to the harp
It is the song of the fly that makes the night to love
The sky that has stars that are not lit
Even the months don't burn enough
But in the dark her/his face shines
I go forward, and ask for a dance
Extend my hand
Even though I don't know which step to take
Follow the song, it will take you there
The words of my brother, concerned but, I am not afraid of anything
I trust myself a little, I am lost right now
Close my eyes so that I am assured that I am not dreaming
I am breathing...

Translated from the Zulu original – Isibindi – *by Innocentia Mhlambi*

Kwahlongasibi
Zulu

Uyise ubehluleka ukumtshela
Ubeyisa engatshelwa
Ikhanda limtshela okwakhe
Ubeyisala kutshelwa uZenzile.
Kuyamangaza ukubona nimkhalela uma esopha.
Enkundleni yababhubhayo
Kugcwele abafuna ukubizwa ngezikhokho
Kungumqansa ukukhalima abafowethu
Uma sebekitazwa yizinto zakamhlaba.
Baya nganxane bengemanzi
Beholwa yinxano,
Sebeyocwila kwamponjwana.
Kwahlongasibi
Yisiphetho samahlongandlebe.
Isimo sibi.
Akekho uzumekile uma niya ngobuso emlilweni bant'abasha.
Lendlela eniyihambayo kayiyintsha
Indala ubufakazi yinani labaphelela kuyo.

Ungenciki ekuqondeni kwakho
Okugwegwile,
Ubuhlakani buncelwa ezincwadini
Esandleni sakho sokunene ufumbethe
Ubude bezinsuku zakho.
Inkinga uxhawulana kakhulu nezinto
Zobumnyama ezicisha inhlansi
Yengomuso eliqhakazayo.

Kuneziyalo ezidukisayo.
Ezisongoza
Ngaphansi kolimi lontanga,
Uma
Bekhohlisana.
Bakhomba indlela sakuyazi
Beholelana ophathe
Juba bayokuqhutha phambili

Imphimbo yabo imumethe amathuna.
Amaphimbo abo anolibofuzo lwasemalibeni
Ungabalaleli.
Hamba ngokucophelela
Uma ulandela umkhondo oya
eKhenana elikhephuzela amakhekheba ezinyosi.
Uju luyajulukelwa sebenza!

Nyathela kancane.
Izigi zakho zinomsindo kwabanomona.
Baphilela ukuphazamisa abaphikelele empumelelweni.
Baphimisa izinkulumo ezihlose ukubulala
Ik'sasa usalicabanga namhlanje.

Uzophenduka inyumba yamaphupho
Uma uphika namaphika nkani
Kwahlongasibi yisiphetho samahlonga ndlebe.

Nokuhlwa bekuhluleka ukumqoqa
Seze waqoqwa ukufa kwamfaka endlini

Yokugcina
Ngoba alikho igumbi ebengalazi endaweni
Ubesephumile yena esandleni.
Nginamahloni ukufunda umlando kamufi.

NTOBEKO LETHU NKWANYANA

At the Place of Those Who Will Not Be Faulted

His father failed to talk to him
He was insolent not heeding to anyone
He only listened to his senseless head
He refused to listen he was Zenzile, the self-inflictor.
It is surprising to see everyone pitying him when he gets his comeuppance.
In the field of die-hards
Where there were those who wanted to be known for their bad ways
It is a mountain warning our brothers
When they are tickled by the pleasures of this world.
They flow to one side like water
Lead by thirst,
When drowning in alcohol.
At the place of those who will not be faulted
Is the end of those who lack ears
The situation is bad.
There is no claiming ignorance when approaching fire face first.
The route you are travelling in is not new
It is old the witness is the number of people whose end is in it

Don't depend in your understanding
Of the crooked,
Wisdom is sucked from books
On your right-hand side you are holding
The length of your days.

The problem is you shake hands too much with things
Of the dark that put out the light
Of your bright future.

There are instructions which are misleading
That lurk
Underneath the tongue of peers
When
Fooling one another
They point the direction as though they know
Leading one another astray
Dove they will fleece you ahead along the way

Their voices are embodying graves
Their voices have the DNA of the grave
Don't listen to them
Go ahead cautiously.
If you follow the path that go
To Canaan that is overfilled with combs of honey
Honey is hard to get work hard

Step slowly
Your steps are too loud for the jealous ones
They live just to disrupt those who are focused on success
They utter speeches aimed at killing
The future you thinking about today.

You will be transformed to the barren dreams

If you align yourself with self-destructive people
At the place of those who are not faulted is the end of those who lack ears.

Dusk failed to gather him
But death eventually gathered him and returned him inside
His final house
Because there was no room he did not know in the neighbourhood
He had gotten out of hand
I am ashamed to read the obituary of the deceased

Translated from the Zulu original – Kwahlongasibi – by Innocentia Mhlambi

Ibali Lami Abalazi
Zulu

Noma ngingababalisela ngebali lami kuyefana
bazongehlulela.
Kubalisa intombazanyana encane,
Izinyembezi zichichima emehlweni.
Ikhala ibalisa usizi ne nhlupheko kulotshwe kuyo
emehlweni.
Ikhala ibalisa ngokuhlukumezeka kanye,
Nobunzima esidlule kubona isencane nakangaka.

Ithi kimi izinsizi zayo zikhule zidlula iminyaka enayo.
Nokuphila isiyaphila nje ngoba kulicala emazulwini
ukuzithathela umphefumulo.
Kwathi isabalisa ngebali layo
Kwahela ngoba nami ngibaliwe esifazaneni.
Ngakhetha ukuhlala phansi ngilalele
Ingibalisela ngebali layo intombazanyana.

Slindile ngihlukunyezwa ngubaba ongizalayo.
Ngicela uma ulizwa lonke ibali lami ungangehluleli.
Indawo ebengihlala kuyo ngiyesaba nokuyibiza ngekhaya
Kuleliyakhaya selokhu kwahamba engizalayo intokazi
Ngaphendulwa inyamazane ngubaba ongizalayo.
Mangike ngavela emehlweni kababa ngisitheliswa
ngezinqindi nezibhakela.

Nalosisi ahlekisana naye ubaba, mangikhala kuye
Uthi ezomndeni akazingeni
Ngiyamangala ngoba wakwazi ukuba ngowesine
kulomndeni

Nomama naye wahamba akaphindanga wabheka emumva
Sengisola nokuthi bamuphendula ngama khathakhatha
Uthule uthini ngithukwa nge gama lakhe.

Slindile ngiyasola laba bobabili banesandla ekushoneni
kukamama
Ithi kimi nokudayisa ngomzimba sekuyisinqumo sayo.
Ithi kimi incono lempilo eyiphila manje kuneyasekhaya.
Uma abantu bengihleka angibasoli
Ibali lami abalazi.

SLINDILE NQASHI

They don't know my story

Even though I tell them of my story it is just the same, they will judge me.
Complained a little girl,
Her eyes streaming with tears.
Crying sorrow and poverty written in her eyes
Crying complaining about the trauma and
The hardship she has gone through even at her tender age

She says to me her sorrows are bigger than her age.
The fact that she is alive it is because it is a sin to take one's life.
It was when she was recounting her story
I felt pain because I am a woman too
I chose to sit down and listen
To the girl telling me about her story

Slindile, I am molested by my biological father
I am asking that when you hear my story don't judge me.
The place I stayed at, I am afraid of calling it home
In this house ever since my mother went away
I was turned into prey by my biological father.
Whenever father saw me he beat me up with fists

Even this lover of my father, when I cry to her
She says she will not be drawn into family matters
I am surprised because she was willing to be the fourth one in this family
And mother left without ever looking back
I suspect they bewitched her

Why would mother be quiet when I am insulted through her name.

Slindile I suspect these two have a hand in mother's death
She says to me selling her body is her decision.
She says the life she leads now is better than the one at home
When people laugh at her, she does not blame them
They don't know my story.

Translated from the Zulu original – **Ibali Lami Abalazi** – *by Innocentia Mhlambi*

Isicelo Somntwana
Xhosa

Liphum'ilang'evuya ezele yimihlali
Ngob'umntwan'uvuyiswa nayintw'engeni, akanangxaki
Entliziyweni yakhe kuzel'uxolo nothand'olumhlophe
qhwa!
Ulindel'inkuseleko nenkathalo kuwe ke Mzalikazi
Ulind'ubushushu nothando kuwe Tata!
Sinye jwi isicelo somntwana kweli lizwe!
Ilizwe elaphelelwa yinimba kwanini!
Ilizwe elambeth'ingub'emnyama yenkohlakalo!

Mkhangele ebukubukwana ebukeka okwengelosi!
Liphum'ilanga evuya ethakazel'engenaxhala
Atsiba tsib'evuyiswa nayintw'engeni umntwana
Akazi ukuba lingatshon'ekobandayo ethe cwaka!

Akaz'ukuba kukhw'izibhongobhiyane ezinxanelwe igazi
Gxebe ezingoyikiyo ukuchith'igazi ngenxa yemali!
Kwowu! Yayaphi na inimba mabandl'akaNtu!
Kwakha kwashishinwa na ngomntu zinkosi?
Umntu! Umntu kaThixo ! Igugu!

Abantwana bethu baphil'okwamantshontsho eenkukhu!
Ezikolweni kanti nasekhaya kudakas'utshaba
Ezindleleni luyandanda phezu kwab'okokhozi
Abantwana bethu badlala phandle bevundlile
Kunzim'ukuthemba nditsho nabegazi
Sinye jwi isicelo somntwana lusapho lwasekhaya
Yinkuseleko yobomi!
Luthando olungenankohliso nantiyo!

Ezi mveku zibiwayo ngamaqhawe esizwe lawo!
Ezi ntsana zibiwayo ngamathemba aza kumisa iAfrika
ngomso
Ezi ntsana zibhaqwa entlabathi zingasenabomi, ngabazali
bangomso
Kwowu! Bayiphin'ubuntu manene ndiphenduleni?
Anisa sikwa nayi nimba nani na manenekazi?

Sinye jwi isicelo somntwana kweli lizwe
"Sikhuseleni bazali asinathemba limbi,
Sijonge kuni nekamva lethu likuni
Njengomsonto bujinga phambi kwenu ubomi bethu"

Lusizi! Yintlungu kumzal'ozeleyo
Kanti nongazelanga kaloku igazi liyajiya kunamanzi
Khanize sithethe kaloku basind'abantwana
Bazali yizani nani zihlobo nabamelwane!
Makubuy'ubuntu zidake zitshabalal'iintliziyw'ezimbi
Ezi yimiwonyo yengqumbo kuba zigcwel'inkohlakalo
Babizwa kancinci baqhathwe ngentw'emnandi
Bakhohliswa ngoncum'olufana nolwengcuka, bathi pheselele
Ancum'umntwana kub'uthanda ngobunyulu
Ad'athande nalowo uzimisel'ukumgwaza
Kub'uthando lomntwana lumpululuswa
Lucwengile! Alunasibi!
Phuthumani Ubuntu ma-Afrika!
Khanilunge! Khuselan'abantwana bezwe lethu!
Eso sisicelo somntwana ngamnye kweli lizwe.

ZUKISWA ZUKI PAKAMA

A Child's Request

The day began with her being happy and rejoicing
Because a child is made happy by the smallest of things, and has no problems
Her heart is filled with peace and love as pure as snow
She is expecting care and protection from you, Mother
She is expecting warmth and love from you, Father
There is only one request from a child in this country!
A country that no longer has love for a child
A country covered by a black blanket of cruelty

Look at her little fat cheeks looking like an angel
The sun rising with her, she's happy and not worried
The child jumping around, made happy by the smallest things
Unaware that the sun could set with her in the cold, and dead!

She does not know that there are predators who have a thirst for blood
Fearless monsters who are not afraid to spill blood for money!
Alas! What happened to conscience, Africans!
Since when do we ever trade a human being, folks!
A human being! God's very people! Pride!

Our children are living lives of hen's chicks !
At schools and homes enemies are on the prowl
On the roads it hovers like over them
Our children play outside with caution

It is even hard to trust family members
There is only one request from a child, that's to have the family at home
A protector for life!
It is love that has no falsity and curses!
These infants who are being stolen are heroes of the nation!
These babies who are stolen are the hope that will build Africa tomorrow
These babies found in the wilderness and lifeless, are parents of the future
Alas! What happened to ubuntu gentlemen answer me?
Aren't you struck by motherly instincts anymore ladies?
There is only one request of a child in this country:
"Protect us parents we have no other hope to turn to"
We look to you and our future is with you
Like a thread our lives hang before you

It is sorrow! It is painful to a parent that has born children
Even to those who do not have children blood is thicker than water.
Come closer let's talk so that the children can be saved
Parents, friends and neighbours come along!
Bring back ubuntu and let the bad hearts be destroyed
These ones are the pits of anger and are full of cruelty
They are called on softly and given some goodies to fool them
They are deceived with a smile like that of a hyena, and they perish
A child will smile as it loves innocently

And even love the one that is willing to stab her
Because a child's love is pure
It is pristine! It has no fault!
Fetch, Ubuntu Africans
Fix yourselves! And protect the children of our nation
This is a request of every child in this country.

Translated from the Xhosa original – Isicelo somntwana – *by Innocentia Mhlambi*

Handewas
Afrikaans

Ons hande is ons eie nou, dis om't
ewe: in skuld of onskuld was ons
hulle, in vergifnis vertroetel die een
die ander in die ekstra water, om vorme
asof daar klei is en iets gaan lewe
kry, tot ons onthou die langer tyd aan
handewas gewy is uit vrees: dis ons
verborge wens om hulle te oorhandig
in die groet, die greep, die beklinking
van die transaksie, die wêreld in te laat
vaar om alles oor te vat, met ons vingers,
die dosyne beentjies, die vel oopgesprei
met ons kolonies krioelende animalkules
in die palms, ontelbaar en onstuitbaar
soos die sterre bokant ons, die hemele
wat ons hande na bo eens wou loof

HANS PIENAAR

Washing hands

Our own they are now, we wash our
hands, in innocence or guilt makes
no difference, the one fondles the other
forgivingly, in the extra water, with hints
of forms as if they were clay and life will
Soon emerge, until we recall, more time
devoted to washing hands is out of fear:
that our hidden wish is to hand them on
in the greeting, the grip, the striking
of the deal and let them break away
into the world to take over, our fingers,
the dozens of little bones, the spread skin
crawling with our colonies of animalcules
In the palm, countless and relentless
like the stars above us, those heavens
our hands were raised in praise to once

Translated from the Afrikaans original – **Handewas** – *by Pieter Odendaal*

Sunflower smile at the sun

Spring rain this year mingles with so many tears
fields ploughed by countless armoured columns
last year's stubble burned by hyperbaric blasts

Fields well fertilised by young men's blood
And so many, many bodies
bodies more suited to loving than dying

Indiscriminate sickles
careless, and uncaring, bring in the harvest
scythe women and children

No harvest festival, no decorated churches
no grateful hymns, no girls in floral dresses
no dancing in the barn, just the wind lamenting

there will be no sunflowers this year

FERDIE ROBERT SCHALLER

Saturday afternoon

"It's a beautiful afternoon here at Murrayfield
Scotland away to our left, France on our right
60 000 bathed in bright sunlight"
The sun has set over Ukraine

The whistle a wailing air-raid siren
20 000 stumble down the road
past hopelessly snarled vehicles
stepping over abandoned lives

"the crowd roars, the match gets underway"
mothers weep almost silently, toddlers wail loudly
grandparents totter along, cursing everyone in general
– the snow turns to sleet

"Man United have taken the field against Watford
In what promises to be a cracker of a game"
A blind missile dives, two children die
No ambulance sirens – just the collective howl of refugees

"High in the stands the piper plays
rousing the crowd to song"
a mother on her knees holds her dead baby
 curses the world

"halftime at Anfield in an absorbing game" – 100 000 kettles
go on
a priest gives last rites at the side of the road

a young soldier is vaporised blowing up a bridge –
no summer wedding now

"a knock-on, overambitious, the crowd groans"
A javelin strikes a tank, five souls extinguished by incineration
Five families get a notification
Rasputin rages
Washington and NATO express their grave concern,
 send best wishes and prayers
the crowds stream home, Scotland lost, Man U drew.
A beer and a pie
Just another Saturday afternoon.

FERDIE ROBERT SCHALLER

Khuveth' oluvuth' umliloulu
Zulu

Mlil' ovuthe kwelamaShayina
Wabhebhetheka wantantatheka
Wawel' imifula nemichachazo
Waval' amazwe nezikhumulo
Kwadidek' izaz' eNtshonalanga,
Nezinjulalwazi zosolwazi,
Zashayana ngamakhanda zithungath' ulwazi.

KwelamaNtaliyan' ufike wabhubhisa
KwelamaNgisi wafike wangqongqisa
Waqoth' imbokodo nesisekelo
Nkalo zonke kwaqhum' isililo
Kwasal' izinkedama nomlotha womlilo
Kwas' ekusen' imingcel' ivalwe ngci!

Ziwakhiphil' amashob' ezaseNtshonalanga
Zachith' amathambo zadl' imbumba
Zakhiph' imibhemis' ezaseMpumalanga
Bayinyemfisa bayihlehlisa /
Indab' inetulo elidukis' indalo
Basho njal' abazi zonk' indaba.

Nakwelengabad' ufike qathatha
Wadla silaza, wadla fumuka
OkaRamaphosa wahlab' umkhosi
Awuhlab' awulawula namakhosi
OkaKhabazela wabhul' umlilo
Kwanhlanga zimuka nomoya

Sikhuluma nje sisemgonqweni
Emgonqweni wemvalelwakhaya
Sikhuluma nje kuxaben' ubendle
Kuxaben' ubendle Khuvethe ndini!
Le ndaba yomnokoloto iyindab' egudwini
Kudel' owaziy' iyozala nkomoni.

Nyakanyaka ndin' uliqhathil' ilizwe
Uqhekeko lwadl' ubhedu kude naseduze
Kuyangenwa kuyaphunywa
Kuyabanjwa kuyayekwa
Nakhu sithi kuyehla kanti kuyenyukela
Thina sith' awusabonwa, wena uthi n'qambe n'shilo!

Awachithwe la manzi, ayikho le nkukhu.
Pho siyolanyulelwa ngubani na?
Yikon' ukuzifihl' entendeni yesinamandla
Nokuholw' endleleni ngonamandla
Nokuhlal' ethemben' elingamandla
'Ze sikhuseleke nakule mbubhiso.

BONGEKA BUHLE SELEPE

Pandemic that burns wildly

Fire that burnt from the land of the Chinese
That ran wild and torched
That crossed rivers and brooks
That closed nations and ports
The scientists of the West were confused
Even the philosophers of knowledge
Hit their heads against one another trying to find knowledge.

In the land of the Italians you arrived there and massacred
In the land of the English you arrived there and burnt everything down
Killing all high and sundry
From all hemispheres there arose great wailing
Only orphans were left behind with ashes
In the morning the borders were closed

In the West they started divining
They poured down the bones and thought
In the North, they took out snuff
They weakened it and pushed it back
The cause is in the myths that led nature astray
They say so those who know all matters.

Even in this country of our birth you arrived
You gobbled up all and sundry
Ramaphosa issued out a warning
The chiefs took it up
Dr Mkhize fought the fire
Nonetheless his attempts failed

As we speak we are quarantined
Quarantined of home lockdowns
As we talk things are bad
Things are bad with the pandemic
This matter of lockdowns is on everyone lips
Only God knows how it will all end

Confusion you have caused infighting within the nation
Fracture is all over far and near
Some are getting in others are leaving
Attempts are made but only to be left half way through
As people we think things are getting better whereas they are becoming worse
We say you have disappeared, and you say I am still alive and kicking

Let us throw in the towel
But then who will mediate for us?
It is hiding yourself in the hand of the most powerful
And to be led on the road by the most powerful
And to remain in the most powerful hope
So that we are saved from this destruction

Translated from the Zulu original – Khuveth' oluvuth' umliloulu – *by Innocentia Mhlambi*

Mncedisi Baldwin Shabangu
Sepedi

Thaba ya bodiragatši o e nametše diloka o tloša
O gata melaba phefo tša phelo bjo di foka
Bjalo ka mabele a sekgowa o hlokola dihloko
Papadi e le ya go bea senkgwa makaleng a tafola
Dithama mekotikoti boka seragathethotsoko
Mola lago lesego e le lekepekepe šebešebe
Pitša o fehla ya bobete ntle ga go fela pelo
O re go fehla o phušula mangoti
O sena taba gore o gadika ya mphodi
Thutophahlošo o aba tša go thenkgolla dilabi mahlong a difofu
Bohlale e le bja go šupa tau malomelo
O le bjalo ka mabele o kwetše komelo
Gare tadi e amuša wa raga kgamelo
Wa ba kgobokanya ka difela le dikopelo
Princess Khanysha ka mogobo a re hlokiša kotselo

Mnce!
Baditšhaba ba sa gakanegile
Ba ipotšiša gore o antše la mohuta mang
Ge mola bontši ba antše la nthorobela
Gwa fulara wena dikgomo tša timela
Modiši wa kgomo o gitla sa borare ijoo!
Megokgo e fegolloga makaleng a sefahlego
O re ge nkabe re di bone re be re tla di rogaka
Ra di tshwela ka togotogo ya mare
Ra bušetša letšwa go Mmopi ka bjako
Ra mo kgopela gore nke a refe motsotswana nago
Pele gage ya legodimo phalafala a ka letša

O re šia le mang ge o sepela monna wa Moswatsi!
Naa selepe o rile go rema wa bea kae?
Go reng seširo se tswalela mola mahlo dinameng re sa ntšhitše?
Gwa fulara wena sefala sa hloga lefoka
Moropa wa hunyela lentšu
Ra oretša sekgololo le matikwane letšatši
Modumo wa le šupa le hlabile la marega
Ka ge phiri ya swele e phušutše mmoto re sa kgopha
Re kwele ka thaga go gwadigwatša dithaba ka mararankodi 'a melodi
Ra kwešiša gore sello ke sa bošogošogo.

Moses Seletiša

Mncedisi Baldwin Shabangu

You climbed to the pinnacle of the acting echelon
Rose against hurdles and obstacles
Going an extra mile to sift to pick the best
The name of the play is putting food on your table
Dimpled
Your laughter intoxicating
With patience brewing the best productions
Giving attention to detail
Minding your own business
Your insightful mentorship could restore a blind man's sight
Your wisdom
Maturity
You left for yonder
They gathered with hymns in your name
With a powerful rendition Princess Khanysha gave us sleepless nights

Mnce!
The world is still astounded
They ask who are you
How do you differ from the rest
Why your departure brought a solar eclipse
There's wailing in the land
Tears stream down people's faces
If we foresaw we would have cursed
Spitted upon
Hurriedly returned the spell to the Creator
Begged Him to afford us a few minutes with you
Before blowing His trumpet

Who are we leaving us with beloved Swati patriarch!
What legacy are you leaving us with?
Why does the curtain fall while we anticipate more drama?
Your final bow is how the play ended
The drum was muted
Darkness fell
We saw Winter sun
As you were snatched from us while we enjoyed your craft
We heard it from the chirping of the loerie bird
We understood it was a wailing cry

Translated from the Sepedi original – Mncedisi Baldwin Shabangu – *by Goodenough Mashego*

Se se jeleng rre
Setswana

Rre o ragile kika re sa lebelela,
Rre o ne a lela ka selo mpeng selela,
Selo e ne e se sejeso se ne gana go fela,
Ke gana nyang ya banyana ntse ke lela,
Sejeso se nna ga ke se itsi ka pono,
Kana selo o ka se se gane o sa se bona.

Ke utlwile lentswe le goeletsa,
Lentswe le ene e le selelo,
E ne e le selelo sa go felegetsa,
Ke tlhokile kitso go tsibusa pelo.

Pego e ntsosa ke robetse,
Pelo ya tsibuga e itibetse,
"Monna rrago o re tlogetse,"
Ka itshwara senna kere ke amogetse.

Babegi go tswa ka lebati,
Mogala wa letheka go mme,
Mme go thubega ka selelo,
"Rrago o isitse marapogobeng" a bua mme.

Ke butse matlho ke ga ke bona bontsho,
"Toro e, ga ke e rate" ke bua ke ya fatshe,
Lefatshe lame la gagoga ka bogare,
Leru le le sweu la fetoga bontsho.

"Tota ke mang a jisitseng rre?"
Ke ne ke ipotsa dipotso di sa fele,

Leso ke leso le itlela fela ke amogela,
Mosong ke itlhaba ka ipotsa gape.

Selo se jele rre,
Se ne se betsana leene ka nnoga e tshela,
Se se sa feleng se a tlhola,
Mmutla o seke wa ba rothisa madi,
Se ke khupamarama.

     KAGISO SEJAMOHOLO

What took my father

Dad unexpectedly departed,
He complained about a stomach bug,
It was not sejeso it was incurable,
I protest while crying,
I know not what sejeso looks like,
You can't deny that you haven't seen.

I heard a loud voice,
A cry,
A farewell lament,
I lacked knowledge to warn my heart.

The report jostles me from sleep,
It shocks my heart
"Your Dad has left us"
I composed myself thinking I accepted.

Messengers exit the door,
I called my Mother,
She broke down in tears,
"Your Dad left to his people," she says.

When I opened my eyes I saw darkness,
"I don't like these dreams," I say bending,
My world was torn in two,
A white cloud turned black.

"Who poisoned my father?"
I kept asking myself questions,

Death comes regardless,
I keep asking myself questions.

Something took my father
It fought against him
Everything comes to an end
Everything must be kept under wraps
It is a secret

Translated from the Setswana original – Se se jeleng rre – *by Goodenough Mashego*

Ubomi bakho bobethu
Xhosa

Awukwazi
ukuthatha obomi bakho
kukhathazeke thina
kanti ubomi bakho, bobakho

akwenzeki
ukuba kulimale wena
kube buhlungu kuthi
kanti ubomi bakho, bobakho.

akwenzeki
ukuba kugule wena
kukhathazeke thina
akanti obo bomi bakho, bobakho.

obo bomi udlala ngabo,
obo bomi ufuna ukubuchitha,
obo bomi uzimisele ukubutshabalalisa,
obo bomi, ayibubo obakho

ayibubo obakho, bobalowo:
uzakumshiya edandathekile,
exheleke umxhelo, etyumke intliziyo,
onakele ingqondo wakuba ubuchithile

SIWAPHIWE FORTUNE SHWENI

Your life is our life

You cannot take your life
and leave us to worry.
yet your life, is your life

it is not possible
that you get hurt
and we feel the pain
yet your life, is your life.

it is not possible
that you get sick
and we get worried
yet that your life is, is yours alone.

that life you are playing with,
that life that you want to waste,
that life that you are prepared to destroy,
that life is not your life

it is not your life, it is the life of:
the person you will leave depressed,
wallowing in grief and broken hearted,
with a destroyed mind because you would have spilled it away,

it is the life of the one who: will be hurt
when you are scratched, when you are hurt
they feel the pain on themselves
even when you are the one who is hurt

in your decisions
about your lives
do not think for
yourselves only

let us know of those decisions
think for us also
your lives
are also ours

Translated from the Xhosa original – **Ubomi bakho bobethu**
– by Innocentia Mhlambi

Akazazi
Xhosa

akazazi, ungambuzi ukuba ungubani,
uncede umncede ngakucelayo,
ewe uzawuthi akanabani, kaloku:
usinde kwinzipho zabo ebebazi nje ngosapho,
suke zajik'izinto mhla besiva, bebona ukuba
uzithandela kwabafana naye ngokudalwa,

uphuncuke kwezo nzipho bezimkrwitshel'
ukuba zimombel'ingcwaba zimngcwabe,
isizathu sithi ugcwel'ukungcola,
batyhola ngelithi igama nesidima sosapho
aph'ekuhlaleni sinomsizi, ngenxa yakhe
kaloku naye uzalwa kolusapho.

akazazi, ungambuzi ukuba ungubani,
ungambuzi ukuba uzalwa ngubani
kodwa ndiyakucela, ngelicengayo
uze uncede umncede ngakucelayo

            Siwaphiwe Fortune Shweni

He does not know himself

he does not know himself, don't ask him who he is
please help him with what he asks for
yes he will say that he does not have anybody
he escaped the hands of those he knew as family
they turned on him when they saw
he likes those who are like him

he escaped the nails that were scratching him
digging a grave for him so they can bury him
the reason they say that he is a cruel person
they accuse him of undermining the name and dignity of
the family
it has been stained with mud because of him
Because he is also the member of this family

he does not know himself do not ask him who he is
do not ask who are his parents
but I plead to you
help him with whatever he asks for

Translated from the Xhosa original – **Akazazi** *– by Innocentia Mhlambi*

Sebalibaleka
Zulu

Sebalibaleka,akusakhulunywa ngabo,
Kufanele phela babengeziqhwaga,
Eyabo impi kwakungeyokuxosha ikati eziko,
Ibhebhezelwa izifiso ezinhle ngemindeni yabo.

Sebalibaleka,abasakhunjulwa nhlobo,
Kufanele phela babengande ngamlomo,
Babekhuluma uma kunesidingo kuphela,
Bekhuluma amazwi anentokozo naphilisayo,
Ayevuselela ithemba kwabathandiweyo babo.

Saqhuma isibhamu,
Yasha imizi,
Laphalala igazi,
Zadindiliza izinsizwa,
Zashabalala izifiso,
Achitheka amathemba.

Sebalibaleka akusashiwo lutho ngabo,
Nasohlwini lwamaqhawe abaveli,
Nasezikhumbuzweni ababalulwa,
Namaliba abo awahanjelwa,
Nemindeni yabo ayisanakiwe.

Elabo igazi lachitheka,
Ukuze ezogida phezu kwalo amavaka,
Azitamuzele ingcebo ngokuthanda,
Atuswe ngobuqhawe nangobuqhawekazi.

Sebalibaleka akusashiwo lutho ngabo,
Impi ababeyilwa isadlangile,
Nezifiso ababenazo azikafezeki.

    S<small>ITHEMBISO</small> S<small>IBISI</small>

They have been forgotten

They have been forgotten, no mention of them is made,
Indeed it must be so, they were not bullies,
Theirs was a fight to chase away the cat from the heath
Fuelled by good wishes for their families.

They have been forgotten, erased from memories,
Indeed it must be so because they were not loud-mouths,
They only spoke when there was a need,
They spoke words that brought happiness and which gave life,
They revived hope among those they loved.

The gun exploded,
Homes were razed to the ground,
Blood flowed,
Men were slain to the ground,
Hopes disappeared,
Hopes were thrown out.

They have been forgotten, no mention is made of them,
Even on the list of heroes their names are not there,
Even in commemorations they are not mentioned,
Even their graves are not visited,
Even their families are neglected.

Their blood was spilt,
So that cowards may dance on it,
Greedily eating up wealth with impunity,
Praised for heroism.

They have been forgotten, no mention is made of them,
The war they fought continues apace,
Even the wishes they had have not been fulfilled.

Translated from the Zulu original – Sebalibaleka – *by Innocentia Mhlambi*

Amahlathi Amnyama
Zulu

Sisemahlathin'amnyama khuce,
Kawabhekeki maye ayesabeka!
Sihamba siyababayela, siqhuga njengexhegu,
Sihamba lukeke, sihlatshwe ngamev'enkohlakalo
Sigxiz'igazi lezinyembezi selingamaxhaphozi,
Sibathe senz'izaba,sibhula lomlilo wothathe
Oshis'amafusi nezikhotha zabamnyama,
Izimpisi ezimehl'abomvu ziyahhahhama,
Zithumel'izinsong'ezinyantisa igazi
Zith'umhlab'ubanzi kwagoqanyawo,
Sibathathe phans'emhlabeni wezintuthwane,
Sabaphanyeka phezu kwezihlalo zamakhosi
Kepha sebeyimamb'emnyama kabasabhekeki,
Sekudum'izihlonono zebhodw'eliconsayo
Oke wathi nkente, useyinyathel'emsileni,
Noqhamuka neqhingasu elishay'emhloleni,
Ushayw'indiva njengesichuse sokuthus'izinyoni
Ingan'akabelethang'esibelethweni somtakabani,
Izwi lezinkinsela yilon'elingaconsi phansi
Baligwinya lingenamsoco, balinambitha libaba,
Ngaphesheya komful'iqhakazile iNkomo kaHaga,
Nganeno ibang'umunyu indlu yabampisholo
Phakathi kwabo likhamisil'igebe likaNomcebo,
Eladaleka ngesandla sonya sontamolikhuni
Ababedla bephiphitha phezulu kwelenyoni,
Qede basiphosel'amathambo angenamnkantsha
Lala Thomas Sankara, lala delakufa,
Cambalala Patrice Lumumba egodini lokugcina
Niwaphundlil'amahlath'amnyama khuce,

Lathwas'ihlobo lenkululeko, lavunula ngemisebe
Sahub'uNkosi Sikelela i-Afrika kaEnock Sontonga
Ihubo elal'umbanis'owengabadi nowaseNtshona,
Kepha sisabhekene nomqans'ongakhwelwa mbongolo,
Kusebuqamama kuleziya zintab'eziluhlaza cwe
Kepha siyogiya sihlab'usentu simpongolozeze,
Mhla kwabuy'ifagugu lomhlab'owalahlekayo
Mhla sashiyelan'umbel'ogwansile nongxiwankulu,

                                                                        PETROS SIPHO

Black forests

We are in the pitch black forests
Very difficult to look at, very frightful!
We move along cautiously, we are limping like an old man
We go sideways we have been pierced by evil thorns
We have been crying blood it has pooled
All our attempts to stomp out the wild fire
Burning the bushes and fields of black people
Red-eyed hyenas are howling
Sending blood-curdling threats
Saying there is plenty of space at the place of the dead
We took them from the ground the realm of ants
And placed them in the highest chairs of kings
But they have turned to black mambas, we are afraid to look at them
Only maddening sounds of pots are overspilling
Once you open your mouth, you would have invited trouble
Even those coming with successful solutions
Are ignored like a scarecrow
Aren't they are not at the backs of important people
The voice of the rich is the one that never touch the ground
They swallow it without nutrition, they taste it even if it is bitter
Across the river the Cow of Haga is bright
This side of the river sorrow is the house of natives
Between them the cliff of Nomcebo has wide open mouth
It was created by the evil hand of racists
Who ate spitting high above in realm of birds
Thereafter they threw marrow-less bones to us
Rest in peace Thomas Sankara, rest in peace revolutionary

Take your rest Patrice Lumumba in your last hole
You have cleared the darkest forest
The spring of freedom came into being, and the sun shone bright with its rays
We sang Enoch Sontonga's Nkosi Sikelel'iAfrika
The song that reconciled natives and westerners
But we are faced with an uphill even a donkey will not climb
The greener mountains are still far away
But we shall dance and issue out a challenge
The day we are returned our heritage of land that we were dispossessed
The day we are given the protruding udder by the powers that be

Translated from the Zulu original – Amahlathi Amnyama – *by Innocentia Mhlambi*

Umzingisi Akanashwa
Xhosa

Zineth'il'izichotho, Kodwa Waluwela Ulwandle
Zigquthil'izaqhwithi, Kodwa Wayiwel'intlango
Ubhabhile NamaKhozi, kodwa Awunazo Neempiko
Njenge Roma, Ubomi Bakho Abukhiwanga Nge Min'enye.

Siyazidla Ngawe Uyiphakamisil'impumakoloni
Bekungelula Ubila Usoma
Ulithemba Kwaye Ungumqondiso
Ukuba Sonke Sizimisele, Sakuyicul'indumiso.

Ukubonil'ukukhanya Ekupheleni Ko Mqolomba
Ngezakh'izandla Impumelelo Wayomba
Wawujikelez'umhlaba, Ungowo didi olukhul'umdlali weqonga
Usikhulisile, Ngokwe Ngqondo Usondla
Ngalo Mbongo Sakuhlala Sikubonga Sisithi
Umzingisi Akanashwa!!!

Lazola Leon Sukula

He Who Perseveres Has No Misfortune
Tribute to Nomhle Nkonyeni

There were heavy storms, but you crossed the ocean
There were wind storms, but you crossed the desert
You flew with eagles, but you have no wings
Like Rome your education was not built in one day

We are proud of how you have uplifted the Eastern Cape
It was not easy sweating from your brow
You were hope and an example
That if all are determined we will sing a praise song

You saw light at the end of the tunnel
With your own hands you dug your success
You travelled the world, you were the star of actress of theatre
You raised us, and fed our minds
With this ode we will always thank you and say
She who perseveres has no misfortune!!

Translated from the Xhosa original – **Umzingisi Akanashwa** – *by Innocentia Mhlambi*

Defiling Stone

Each morning we come to the wall naked. We don't remember
our dreams from the night before. Some say men swam
with dolphins, beached themselves, bouquets of ambergris,
on the shoreline of villages they'd left long ago.
Some say women – pillar, post, corridor – stood in torrential rain,
conjuring stews out of scraps. Some say there was always theys
that channelled the clench of a fist, root of a womb.
Each morning we rumour about the night, waiting for sunlight
to pierce brick, and show which holes need deepening.
With palette knives in knuckled hands, pickaxes in petite fingers,
we move mortar from its hovel. Bricks singly fall at our feet.
The dust of our deconstruction whispers of strait-jacketed stories
impressed upon our bodies. Tales that offer every hunter his prey,
shrouding prey behind veils of prayer. This wall is a palimpsest,
overwritten by men that made roads out of mountains; overwritten
by long-haired women pulling muscled hearts out
of their cages, leaving them powdered in dowry boxes. Overwritten

by the theys – the slipping-in/slipping-out of butch, fem,
Whitney-Houston-Arnold-Schwarzenegger theatre.
Each generation has added to the scribble. Each has
defaced the wall.
Out of three-tiered cakes women drew hammers, hard-
hats, blueprints
for skyscrapers. Out of bonfires of burning suits, men
summoned trains
 of flowing fabric, lassoing headlights, casting soft shadows
on their anuses.
Now, atop the towering wall, theys dance on the parapets,
between the cannons,
drawing us toward their magic trick: convergence.
Come, they say, climb. Taste this new manna on offer.
It is untethered from the bullwhip of pounded-blessed
books.
Only the most agile dare scale this barricade; along the way
some
pick up lipstick, hormones, virtual reality, implants.
Along the way, men bear seahorses in their bellies
 and women sharpen tulips into spears, angling amber piss
into gardens.
And still, theys beckon, describing what's beyond
the wall. A river made of words, they say. And houses
headed
 by revolving doors, where man and woman swing free of
meaning.
 For beyond the wall the body comes home, whole
and malleable, like the atmosphere that surrounds it.

We at the bottom don't believe our ears. We still drill into the spaces
the sunlight reveals, trusting these hands. We know we have to do this
 together. Walls will collapse once broken through.
Survivors must be found in the rubble, cleaned and carried off
to the river. Where the sodden banks of grammar give
 to the quickening current of bodies taking flight
where no wall can claim property of feeling. Where no border
crossed spells exile, and all our longing – lost.

JARRED JAMES THOMPSON

Amagwala
Xhosa

Iyhoo, ndiyindindi
Tshooo, yingxubakaxaka
Kanti yintoni igwala?
Kanti anje amagwala?
Nqandan'amagwala.

Ubugwala sisifo esibi
Lento umntu ngathi akazi
Lento umntu ngathi akafuni
Lento umntu ngathi akanakho
Kanti uyaxoka

Ubugwala ngumbulalazwe
Lakhula inani lobulawa
Lenyuka nelodlwengulo
Kwanda norhwaphilizo ezweni
Zaphinda phinda izijwili esizweni

Aphi amadoda okwenyani?
Baphi abafazi boqobo?
Siqhayise ngonyana bethu?
Sizidle ngentombi zethu?
Hayini magwala

Kodwa magwala niyakhohlisa
Niyatyhafisa nangoku
Niyasihlazisa isizwe
Kutheni ningadani nje?
Zifuneni, guqukani nizohlwaye

Anifuni kwenza
Kodwa niyonzakalisa
Anithethi
Kodwa bayaphela abantu
Magwala ndini mxim.

MBULELO TSHOFELA

Cowards

Yhoo! I am
Tshoo, the confusion
What is a coward?
Cowards are like this?
Stop the cowards

Cowardice is a bad disease
This thing of pretending as though they do not know
This thing of pretending as though they don't want to
This thing of pretending as though they don't have
When they are actually lying

Cowardice is the destroyer of the nation
The rate of those killed increase
Even that of rape increase
Corruption is increasing
Cries of sorrow are repeated throughout the nation

Where are real men?
Where are real women?
Should we brag about our sons?
Should we be proud about our daughters?
No cowards

But you cowards are deceitful
You drain energy even now
You embarrass the nation
Why are you not disappointed?
Search yourselves change and judge yourselves.

You do not want to do
But you hurt
You don't speak
But people are being finished
You cowards

Translated from the Xhosa original – Amagwala – *by Innocentia Mhlambi*

An Eastern Cape Litany

Give us this day our daily water
>without burst pipes, broken pumps or empty dams.

Give us safe passage
>over roads riddled with potholes.

Give us light
>when the streetlights fail.

Grant us a quiet night
>undisturbed by the roar of generators or guns.

Grant us peace
>and spare us from xenophobic outbreaks.

Grant hope to those
>who are forced to protest for basic services.

Guard our children
>in their crumbling schools.

Guide our leaders
>if such people even exist.

And give peace
>to a province in pieces.

CRYSTAL WARREN

Ndirhalela Sikhe Sibaliselane
Xhosa

Ndirhalela sikhe sibaliselane ngezanto zikwenza ungalali
Khawundixelele man kusuke kuthini?
Ucinga ntoni kangaka mntwanomntu?
Ingaba ucinga le mpilo kaIna-ethe?
Ucinga ezinzame zingenamvuzo?
Mfondini sihlala sihlakuhlakula sihl'amahlongwane
phezulu!

Akhonto ingenayo zonke ziyaphuma
SikwiShinini elingena ngeniso, sixhathisile!
Sityibilika sisiya mntakwethu sibetheka ngemilomo
Kwiingcango esicinga zizovuleka, kutheni mna ndedwa
Ndasoloko ndabetheka elityeni ngentloko?
Kutheni le ntando yalomfo ingakhe ingqamane neyam?

Ndiziva ndixineka kwakurhatyela, ndixinwa ziingcinga
ezingephi, ndiziva ndidadela enzulwinini mntase
Ndingarhaxwa nanini kuba andiwathembanga lamandla
ndinawo, khandibalisele!
Ndiyakuxelela elaa qhosha lisesifubeni lakukhululeka
Andikuqinisekisi ngasisombululo kodwa xa ungekho
wedwa kwezingxubakaxaka

Uyakuziva ngcono kuba xa sibaninzi ayinakukuxaka
Thetha nam sthandwa, phungula zonke ezongxaki zakho
Kulefatyi yam, khumbula lefatyi isenqwelweni ehamba
ngamavili omthandazo, asithethi ngaOli iluhlaza apha!
Uzovakalisa iintlungu zakho kuSombawo ucele izinto
Ezime endleleni zisuduke, konk'okuhle kuze kuwe

Izinto zilunge, izingqi zakho umthyoli azibhude
Ubumnyama busuke, amathuba namathamsanqa akuchule
Ndirhalela sikhe sibaliselane ngezanto zikwenza ungalali,
Khawundixelele maan kusuke kuthini ucinga ntoni
kangaka mntwanomntu?Ndiyakuthembisa andizukwenza
vangeli ngentlungu yakho kwiimbutho
Zabagxeki, ndifuna nje sijike lamava akho abeyimfundiso
kwabanye
Mhlawumbi nesilumkiso.

ZUSAKHE RHASATSHA ZIDE

I wrote this for you

I wrote this for you, versifying revelations and secrets while constructing
A sensible operation of the mind.
Because I've got connections, I'm the postman delivering letters from Heaven,
The letters contain a basket of surviving material for your path.
I wrote this for you introducing your emotional armour, I carry words of wisdom
At the palm of my hand, I carry messages from both underground resistance and
Celestial city and as young as I am I can show you life in three dimensions.

So give me the puzzle, from the letters we can find the missing piece.
Show me the knot, from the letters we can learn how to disentangle it.
I'm telling you! Using the letters we can decipher all the codes of life.
Tell me of the depression that whispers horrible music in your ears!
Tell me of the anxiety attacks and their triggers, tell me how much you've gotten
To hate bed time.

I wrote this for you

I wrote this for you!

Translated from the Xhosa original – **Ndirhalela Sikhe Sibaliselane** – *by Innocentia Mhlambi*

Erenkini
Xhosa

AkukhoseGoli kwaNdonga-ziyaduma kuphaya Erenkini.
Yithi ndikuxelele ngokuthi singene nzulu kwintlalo aserenkini,
Sibengathi singababhexeshi beenkqubo sazecaweni iyiqale ekuqaleni sibulise oo Nostendi, Hallelujah ooAlpha and Omega,
Iziqalo neziphelo zosuku lwaserenkini, iintatheli ezidiza iindaba
NjengoLisakhanya Pepe sele zinongiwe ziilithsele.

Masingene ezingcanjini zentlalo yabo, ngamabanjwa phaya Erenkini,
Nemali ayisangeni njengakuqala, bantyumpantyumpeka ematyaleni
omgalelo ukanti basantywila nasematyaleni amatikiti ecawa.
Abantwana babo bahleli emiqaleni ngokusoloko benothotho lwezicelo
ezenza ezizi Aram zinyuke iminqantsa zikhobokile, zinyamezele amaqhwa
neemvula zigugile, ndikuxelele ngosizi lwaserenkini.

Bonke esasichopha nabo ezidesikeni zincedisana ukuze singabethwa nguTishalakazi baphelela Erenkini, bonke oonobuhle
bexesha lethu baphelela Erenkini. Ndiyibone ngexesha likaxakeka
ndisexhaleni, kaloku ndiyakwabhidene nalobhuti ubendincedisa ngeempahla

endikhapha, usuke wayiqhwitha wangathi uyolanda indebe yehlabathi.
Ndaqonda mandikhawuleze ndiyomjonga Erenkini!

Xa ndimlaqaza, ndiphefumla onke amavumba andingqongileyo, iizandi
zakulentshukumo zininzi kwaye zahluke ngaxesha-nye.
Uyawuziva ezinye ziduma, ezinye zicima.
Uyawubeva bexambulisana ukuba kulayisha bani,
Uyakuva nemibongo yabathengisi "Isibamule, isihlungu, umhlabelo";
"ngena sisi, ndikwenze intloko Nana?"

Ndizama nje ukubeka phaya Erenkini ukuze umbone untsumpa welashishini.
Isisu sakhe sibhokoxekile ziimali azirhwaphiliza kwabanye abaqhubi,
uzixutha ngesikhundla kaloku abona-bona hlohlesakhe baphaya Erenkini.
Baziwa ngoziqhola ngamayeza enza izimanga, okhe wema endleleni yakhe
ususwa kakubi ngokukhawuleza okudibene nokungxama, kuculwe Unoyana
sele engasayi kuphinda alibeke Erenkini.

Ndithetha ngeziya zihamba zityala iintsana ziduke, emveni kweminyaka
zibuye zivune iziqhamo zeentsana zazo ngo "Ina-ethe" Erenkini.

Bathatha ezaantsana zidingayo zingenza nantoni,
ezisandula kushiywa
ngumama wazo ongazange aliphathe igama likatata.
Tata lowo amphuza umhla nezolo, amfotele iqhekeza
kubekho umgqenya endlini.
AkukhoseGoli kwaNdonga-ziyaduma kuphaya Erenkini.

Zeziya zifike zichophe zibize iplate macala, zitye eqale
yafika bafike sele kusithwa setyile
nabanye abazixakekise ngofudumeza umleqwa.
Zeziya zisibeka kwinqanaba lengabula-zigcawu,
nanjengoko impixano phakathi koosisi
abaphekayo iye intshule, esi sibini size mva siye siqonde
ukuze kulunge makasuke lompheki
Umphefumlo uthathwa okweponti etafileni phaya,
umphefumlo uthathwa lula njengokothula
idyasi emva kocango.

AkukhoseGoli kwaNdonga-ziyaduma kuphaya Erenkini.
Bengavani kanjalo ke, ukuwa komntu baphuma bonke
bayozimasa emgcwabeni, bambi beyele
ukuqinisekisa ukufa qha, bambi beyokujonga kwanto
engaphucukanga ukuze inqanaba eliphala
phambili lize nabo xa kuncokolwa ngobungakanani
besingcwabo.

Bendithetha nomnye wabaqhubi ebik'imbilini yakhe kum
esithi ukuba wenze impazamo encinci
emotweni wangeva xa umkhweli ebiza indawo aphela kuyo,

ufela iizono zabanye abaqhubi
abangenayo imbeko nendlela yokuthetha.
Uthe kum izivubeko azifumana ebahlalini ngenxa
yomsebenzi awenzayo noko ziqatha, akafuni
nokuxoka basile ooNotaxi kodwa bakhona abajonga mntu
ngamnye njengethuba lokubeka
isitya phambi kwabantwana.

UNobuhle weza Erenkini naye engafumani sikolo,
wayenombono wokuthengisa umqolo
neerostile, ngenxa yobutsha bakhe nobuhle bakhe zonke
zamnxanelwa. Wayezokhulisa imali
yobhalisa kunyaka ozayo suka irenki yamfunxa, ngezandla
zozibini yamkhongozela imbukele
edakasa entendeni yayo.
Iziphatha-mandla zabaqhubi zakukhuphiswano lokumfaka
ezingubeni, bonke baphumelela
bemshiya nesinyamfu semali, engayiqondi yena uba
uthengisa ngempilo, ibhanka yakhe izala
ziimali zengeniso neemali zempatho-ntle.

Xa uqala unyaka ubulindiwe, umntwana wakhoboka, ilizwi
elitsala kude. Wayephefumla ngathi
wenza okokugqibela, yayicaca nasesidengeni ukuba
UNobuhle unyathele intambo kwataka
iintlantsi.
AkukhoseGoli kwaNdonga-ziyaduma kuphaya Erenkini.

ZUSAKHE RHASATSHA ZIDE

At the taxi rank

It is not Johannesburg city of gold it is the taxi rank
Let me tell you in detail about life at a taxi rank
Be like preachers in church who are in charge of the programme
first let's start by greeting the Landlords, Hallelujah Alphas and Omegas
The beginnings and end of days at a taxi rank, journalists who share news
Like Lisakhanya Pepe (xhosa news reader) the news are ready.

Let's get to the root of their way of life, they are prisoners there at the taxi rank
Money no longer comes in like before, they are drowning in debt
of their stokvels and they are drowning in debt from their church pledges
Their children are breathing on their necks with their never ending requests
that make these poor people endure climbing hills in chains also enduring snow storms
and rains when they are so aged, I am telling you about the sadness at the taxi rank

All those that we used to sit with in class in desks helping each other so that
we are not beaten by our teacher, all of them end up at the taxi rank all the beauties

of our time end up at the taxi rank. I saw this at a busy time.
I was worried, because I had come across this man who helped me with my luggage
Escorting me, he just lifted it as if he is lifting the world cup trophy
I realised that I should quickly go to the taxi rank to look for him!

When I was busy looking for him, inhaling all the smells surrounding me, the sound
Of the movements is many and different at the same time.
You will hear cars starting other being turned off
You will hear them arguing about who is next to lift passengers
You will hear praises of vendors, "pain killers, incense", "enter sister, can I do your hair nana"

I am trying to paint a picture for you to see the chief who owns the business at the taxi rank
His belly is shaped like a rugby ball (deformed) because of the money he takes away from other drivers
He takes it away from them because he is the boss, the very ones who line their pockets because they are lords there at the taxi rank
They are known for their use of strong medicine on any one who stands in their way
That person is removed badly with a swiftness accompanied by speed, then Noyana songs will be sung
So that he will never set foot at the rank

am talking about those men who will impregnate and disappear
and come back after years to reap the benefits of their children, the "Ina-ethe", at the taxi rank
They take in needy children who are willing to do anything, who have been abandoned by a mother who has talked about the name of a father
A father she kissed every single day and shared pictures with so that there will be food to bring home
It is not Johanneburg the city of gold it at the taxi rank

Those are the type that come sit and order a plate from both sides, eat the first to arrive, then when the other order arrives they will be told that he has already eaten with others who have been warming up chicken
Those are a type that are placed at the level of trouble makers, and cause disagreements between the women that cook to become worse, and those who later come to restore order will realise that so as to correct the situation, one of the cooks must be removed
Life is equated to a pound on the table, like taking a jacket from the back of the door

It is not Johannesburg City of gold it is the taxi rank
As they do not see eye to eye, when a person died, they all go to the funeral to support, some go there to ensure the deceased is dead indeed, others to see to it that nothing important is missed so that the most important point came

with them when they gossip about the size of the funeral
I was talking to one driver who was expressing hist hurt to me, saying that when he makes a mistake by not hearing where the passenger wants to be let off, he will be punished for the sins of other drivers who have no respect and etiquette
He says to me the abuse he gets from residents because of the work he does is too much, but he does not want to lie, taxi drivers/owners are rude even though there are those who look up to people as an opportunity to put food on the table for children

Nobuhle (The Beautiful One) came to the taxi rank as well because she could not find space for school
she had ideas of selling cooked and roast meat, because of her youth and beauty all men lusted after her
She was there to raise money for registration the following year, the taxi rank sucked her in, with both hands welcomed her, watching her parading herself in the palm of its handsv
All the taxi owners competed to get her in bed, all of them succeeded they left her with loads of money, she did not realise that she is selling her life away, she was gaining interest with the money for a soft and pampered life.

When the year began, she was enslaved and her voice was indistinguishable, her breathing was
as if she is taking her last breath, it was clear even to a fool that the beauty has stepped on a trap

And an explosion incurred.
AkukhoseGoli kwaNdonga-ziyaduma kuphaya Erenkini.
This is not Johannesburg city of gold it is at the taxi rank

Translated from the Xhosa original – Erenkini *– by Innocentia Mhlambi*

Uyangiholel' emadlelwen' aluhlaza
Zulu

Uyangiholel' emadlelwen' aluhlaza
Uthembakel' ezweni lakhe
Ungiholel' emadlelwen' ukuba ngiwabone
Ungiholel' emadlelwen' ukuba ngiwabuke
Ungiholel' emadlelwen' ukugcin' okulotshiwe
Keph' ekungiholeni kwakh' akavumi ngidle
Keph' ekungiholeni kwakh' akavumi nginethezeke
Uyangiholel' emadlelwen' aluhlaza
Yize kucac' ufuna ngibon' ubukhulu bakhe
Yize kucac' akafuni ngibuzw' ubukhulu bakhe

NKULULEKO ZONDI

He leads me to greener pastures

He leads me to greener pastures
He is worthy of trust in this world
He leads me to pastures so that I can see them
He leads me to pastures so that I can behold them
He leads me to pastures to confirm what has been recorded
But even as he leads me he does not allow me to eat
But even as he leads me he does not allow me to be comfortable
He leads me to greener pastures
Even though it is clear he wants me to see his greatness
Even though it is clear he does not want me to feel his greatness

Translated from the Zulu original – Uyangiholel' emadlelwen' aluhlaza *– by Innocentia Mhlambi*

Cabanga
Zulu

Cabanga nje! kunjani ukub' esibayeni
esingena nkunzi laph' uhlal' ubona kuphela
inkomanzi namathol' ayo zigenayo insika
umasheq' emuke ngendle njengamabele

yonk' ingane iding' ubaba,
bonk' obaba bading' izingane
ngisho nezindela bezingathand' ukuba
namazibulo nom' amathunjana

inkunz' idliwe yizintaba, amakonyane
acashe kunin' asingathwe ngunina
umasheqe ushiy' isibongo esigenasinanazela
inkunzi azange isabhekis' amaphond' emuva

yafak' umolom' esiqundwin' izidlel' ezikhotheni
amakonyan' azinakazi anothil' esibayeni
ngebis' elinothile ngothando luka mama
umashenqe ukhomba ngophakathi
amokonyane nonina badl' imbuya ngothi

LUCAS DELISIWE ZULU

Think

Just think! How is it to be in the cattle pen
that does not have a bull where you only see
cows and their calves without pillars
the wanderer having gone with waste like sorghum seeds

all children need their father
all fathers need their children
even the nuns would have loved to have
first born or last born children

the bull has been swallowed by the mountains, and calves
are hiding themselves under their mothers, are cared for my
their mothers
the wanderer left a surname without honourific names
the bull never turned its horns to look back

if planted its mouth in the grass heap, and simply ate in the
veld
the calves are happy fed fattened in the cattle pen
with nourished milk with love of the mother
the wonderer is living large
the calves and their mother are poor

Translated from the Zulu original – **Cabanga** – *by Innocentia Mhlambi*

Biographies

Ashley Allard is 21 years old and has been writing for 11 of them. She is a third-year English literature and French language student at Stellenbosch University who hopes to pursue a career in creative writing. Ashley is the assistant editor for South African youth zine *Moyé*, which specialises in promoting young South African creatives. When not writing, you can hear her raving about her favourite books and TV series to anyone who will listen.

Ayanda Billie was born in 1975 in KwaNobuhle, Uitenhage, where he still lives. Founder of a local book club to grow a reading and writing culture in his community, he also facilitates creative writing workshops for the youth. He received his MA in Creative Writing from Rhodes University in 2016. Ayanda is the co-founder of Mandela Bay Bookfair. In 2006 his debut collection of poetry, Avenues of my Soul, was published by Swii Arts. *Umhlaba Umanzi* (Imbizo Arts) is his second poetry collection and *KwaNobuhle Overcast* (Deep South) his third. He has published poems in literary journals like *New Coin*, *Ityhini*, *Carapace*, *Kotaz*, *Timbila* and *Illuminations*. In 2019 he won the South African Literary Award for his isiXhosa collection *Umhlaba Umanzi*. Again, this year his English collection of poetry *KwaNobuhle Overcast* won the South African Literary Award 2021 in poetry category.

Toroga Denver Breda from ǁHui!Gaes/Cape town is a Khoikhoi First Nations kuru-ao-i/ artist and kares-ao-i/ poet who writes to !kham/challenge the |ari/erasure of the

Khoikhoi gowas/language, which was once the language of the wealthiest people on these lands and Khoi stories.

My sisen/work as a queer, two-spirited xoa-ao-i/writer is my ǂurusen/healing, my connection to my Inqua Khoi abogan from the place colonisers called Graaff-Reinet but, most importantly, my KARE/praise to our taradi/Khoi women.

Bruce Sabelo Buhelezi is a Durban-based poet, story-teller and tour guide, who is also a skilled master of ceremonies. His love for poetry and performing started in 2005 while in high school. He uses his love for Afrikan history to create poems and stories that capture one's imagination. Bruce has shared his works on many platforms and stages around the country and beyond. His work was included in the Creative INK Anthology of poems and short stories published in 2008 and launched at the Poetry Africa Festival.

Nompilo Cele is 24 years old and was born in Ndwedwe Kwabhanoyi. She recently obtained an LLB degree from the University of Zululand and a Cultural Media Studies degree from the University of KwaZulu-Natal. She is currently a candidate attorney in a law firm based in Durban. Her work has been published in the all-women poetry anthology, titled *Kuvuka Ingcugce*.

Corné Elizabeth Coetzee's volume *Nou, hier* was published in 2017. Her poems, written from the point of view of a housewife, parent and child of aging parents, they are often about relationships both close and far away as well as social concerns and the environment. Her themes include the inevitable change and eventual disintegration of everything around her. A film and theatre critic, she has written articles for a number of consumer magazines. She is now a sub-editor for Afrikaans newspapers.

Jerome Coetzee is a writer, poet and Master's degree candidate in the Department of Afrikaans at the University of the Western Cape. His research focus is on Afrofuturism in contemporary Afrikaans literature. He has previously been published in *LitNet* and *Die Student*, and is a National Poetry Prize winner (2021). When he is not writing, you can find Jerome at a local poetry reading event with a pen in one hand, a notebook in the other, and always with a cup of tea. In his spare time, he also enjoys mentoring and facilitating online poetry workshops.

Jeremy Peter Dames is a retired educator and poet who graduated from the University of the Western Cape and worked in the Stellenbosch community for almost 40 years. His first book *Stemme oppie Vlakte* (2022) is a collection of his poetry in Afrikaans, for which he received an African honoree authors' award. He was also awarded the honour of being an eTV South-African hero in 2011 for his work with the youth in Stellenbosch. His writing focuses on the social issues and challenges of his community.

Sydney Abraham Davis was born in Retreat on the Cape Flats on 4 April 1948, the son of a fisherman and the second youngest of ten siblings. He attended Thomas Wildschutt Primary and Wittebome High School where his love for poetry was fuelled by two Afrikaans teachers, Mr John Hendricks and Mr Henry Erasmus. After completing his Theological Studies at University of Western Cape, he served as a pastor for 25 years, before entering the NGO sector where he served organisations and communities in the Western and Eastern Cape. He currently resides in Tulbagh and is still involved in community development.

Sihle Dolophini is a poet who grew up in Lady Frere but currently residing in Cape Town. He was a member of Chris Hani Writers Association before he came to Cape Town. He has won a number of poetry slams and competitions including Primpoetry Competition, CA Entertainment Competition and Word is.... Cash Money Poetry Slam. He is also a finalist of Western Cape Provincial Slam and Open Book Festival. He has collaborated with many big artists such as Sivatho Rhigala and Mphozisi Qalekiso. Currently, he is a facilitator of Dira Foundation, which is all about discovering and developing young artists.

Hana Gammon was born in 2002 in Cape Town, and has been passionate about writing for as long as she can remember. She is inspired by peculiar and strangely beautiful elements of the world, and her work is informed by her Christian faith as well as her experiences as an autistic person. During the 2020 lockdown, she decided it was time to start sharing her poetry with the world. She is currently in her second year at Stellenbosch University studying BA Language and Culture. In her free time, she enjoys researching dead languages and sewing historically inspired projects.

Martha Hadebe is a temporary lecturer in the Department of African Languages at the University of Johannesburg. She holds a Bachelor of Education in Senior and FET Phase, a BA Honours degree in African Languages, which she passed with distinction and a Master of Arts in African Languages. She teaches Literature in African Languages and Teaching Methodology and Practicum. She is currently studying towards a doctorate in African Languages.

Shane van der Hoven (they/them) is a radically Kweer poet and feral literary scholar. They are currently reading for their doctoral studies and are teaching poetry translation at the University of Cape Town. They have previously been published in S*tanzas, New Note Poetry, New Coin, Dwelling* and others.

Born in Wartburg KwaZulu-Natal, **Sthembile Thingo Gwala** is a South African Zulu poet, playwright, poetry activist and performer based in Pietermaritzburg. She is also a director and founder of Milando YeMinyaka. She wrote and performed, in collaboration with Phiwokuhle Nyambose, a theatrical series of poems called *SEMBADIH* and a theatre play called *UThingo Shades of Light* in 2014 and 2015. Her poem "UThingo", inspired by the play *UThingo Shades of Light* was featured and published in a 2nd edition of Womandla Poetry Book. "Phola Nhliziyo" is one of her recent poems and it has been selected for Issue #2 of *Paper Trail Literary Journal* which will be released February 2022.

Anathi Jonase or Akhuxolo is a 25-year-old writer who hails from one of the smallest rural settlements at Dutywa known as Upper Falakahla location. He is fascinated by the works in his indigenous language, Xhosa. His words of art seek to heal, educate and comfort the hearts of many.

Sive Joyi is a poet, playwright and actor from Sterkstroom. Currently studying towards a BA degree in Dramatic Arts at the University of the Witwatersrand, he writes in his mother tongue because he believes it has rich idioms and proverbs that can always take him back to the lips of the gods, and thus help him decolonize knowledge. He has performed in poetry slams such as the CSP SLAM (2021) and the TEWOP SLAM (2022).

Lynthia Julius was born in Springbok in 1993 and grew up in Kimberley where she matriculated in 2011. She graduated with an honour's degree in Philosophy from the University of the Free State. She was the 2017 winner of the AVBOB poetry competition in the Afrikaans section for her poem 'Vir Aljarreau'. *Uit die Kroes* (2020, Kwela) is her debut poetry anthology. In 2021 *Uit die Kroes* won the SALA Award for First-time Published Author. Lynthia is currently a Master's student in Creative Writing at the University of the Free State.

Kabelo Duncan Kgatea is PR practitioner with a certificate in Comprehensive Writing, who translates, proofreads and edits Setswana text. He is a two-time winner of the Mnet Book Prize and five-time winner of the Sanlam Prize for Youth Literature in the Sotho languages category. He was awarded the K. Sello Duiker by South African Literary awards (SALA) and the PenSALB Best Setswana Writer and Multilingualism Writer of the Year Award, both in 2009. Through his non-profit organisation Penebotshelo Writers Foundation Kabelo conducts Setswana creative writing workshops. He has authored 12 novels for youth and two drama books, and his work included in many poetry anthologies.

Mpho Peter Khoarai was born on 7 June 1998 in Clocolan, Free State province. After matriculating in 2016, from 2017 he began studying at the University of Cape Town.

Nosipho Samanta Khuzwayo is originally from Ladysmith, KwaZulu-Natal. Nosipho Khuzwayo stands with many titles: poet, songwriter and vocalist. Better known to her fans as Nue-Sam, the artist started writing at a young age and kept honing her craft. It was only in 2013 that she started reciting poems publicly alongside a friend of hers, who was also a reciter and helped in introducing Nue-Sam to a platform of artists.

Hleze Welsh Kunju is a poet, speaker, researcher, actor and musician. He has a BA in Instrumental Music Studies (majoring in Drama & Music) and a BA Honours in African Languages/Music & Musicology (majoring in African Languages, Classical Voice and Orchestral Conducting) from Rhodes University. He also obtained an MA in African Languages/Music and Musicology. He wrote Rhodes University's first isiXhosa PhD thesis and received numerous awards, including "The Most Outstanding PhD Thesis Award by the African Language Association of Southern Africa". Kunju is currently the head of Creative Writing at Rhodes University.

Ntaoleng Patience Labane is from Bloemfontein. Her journey with poetry started in 2018 when she won her first poetry slam (CSP Bloemfontein), after which she went on to win two more slams (Vryfees 2019,UFS). She is the host and founder of "Her Thoughts", which is a podcast celebrating literature, poetry and artists. She's also a visual artist, author, essayist and collector of African Series Writers novels. Her work has been selected to form part of an anthology on African diaspora and women in the technological age by Howard University.

Mmakgotso Annastacia Lehola was born on 5 November 1963 in Kruisfontein-Bothaville. After her schooling, she completed an Intensive Commercial Course certificate, a Business Administration course and an Office Management and Technology course. Currently, she works as administrative clerk at Tshiya DTDC in the Department of Education.

Keith Oliver Lewis is a poet and writer from Paarl. He is the current champion of the National Library of South Africa Poetry Slam Competition. Lewis has shared his poetry on various radio stations, Expresso Morning Show, and performed for local and national online audiences. Two of his poems, "Smartie Town" and "met die sterre gepla" has been published in the collection Yesterdays and *Imagining Realities: An Anthology of South African Poetry*. Lewis is one of the winners of the US Woordfees Short Story Competition.

Nkosinathi Emmanuel Luthuli is budding writer with a consuming passion for poetry, who was born in 1981 in a rural area called Nhloshane. After matriculating in 2001, he obtained a National Diploma and my BTech in Language Practice from the Durban University of Technology. Currently, he works as an Zulu translator. An avid reader, the literary works in Zulu and English of literary heavyweights such as D.B.Z. Ntuli and C.T. Msimang has stimulated his interest to write poems.

Nonceba Mabena was born in Lusikisiki, Eastern Cape and studied at Walter Sisulu University (WSU). Noceba works at the Language Laboratory, WSU, teaching Xhosa sabaQalayo and English for Beginners.

Landisile Magwaxaza was born in Lady Frere and obtained his matric in 1994. He went to Cape Town for greener pastures, and then started writing poetry. He recently published his poetry book titled *Igugu Lesizwe*.

Nolwazi Mbali Mahlangu is a poet with a theatre and performance certificate from the Duma Ndlovu Actor's Academy and is currently part of the Current State of Poetry class of 2020/21. She is the Polokwane Slam Emporium Goddess of the Mic 2018 winner and Ekurhuleni Slam 2018/19 semi-finalist. Her work has been featured on *Confessions*, a Mandla Mpanjukelwa play. She has showcased on 100 Poets for Mandela, 7th Annual Polokwane Literary Fair and the Human Rights Festival at Constitution Hill.

Xolisile Mbali Mabaso was born and raised at Ladysmith and author of the book, *Let's Go My Own*. A member of Vulindlela Writers Club, the founder of I AM MY SISTER'S KEEPER WOMEN EMPOWERMENT, founder of White Rose Events, Xolisile is also a public and motivational speaker.

Tshepiso Makgoloane is a motivational speaker, editor, proofreader, publisher, Law graduate and most of all a multi-award winning author. Her first poetry book won a prestigious South African Literary Award in 2021 in the poetry category. Her other writings have been featured in various literary projects such as *Avbob poetry, Sol Plaatjie European Union Poetry anthologies* (Vols VIII and X) and *Calabash Online Literary Journal* (Vol 3).

Charles Julie Makofane was born in Leboeng, Limpopo. He went to Pitšaneng Primary school and completed his matric at Baroka Secondary School. He then studied for BALP at the University of Venda.

He started writing in 2015 at the age of 18. He has written poetry, short stories and novels. His work was published in *Poetry Lockdown* (2020). His work was also featured in a Northern Sotho poetry collaboration compiled by Mary Madihlabo called *Sa Mafahleng A Rena*. He has worked as an editor and a proofreader on several English and Sepedi books.

Mbali Malimela is a South African Zulu writer, performing poet and storyteller. As a founder of a poetry brand called Bantu Origin, she has a strong passion for restoring the love and use of language through poetry. Mbali has been a part of numerous poetry platforms including the 22nd and 25th Poetry Africa Festival, 25th Time of the Writer Festival, Durban Playhouse Women in Arts Festival and the Artfluence Festival. She has had her writings published in the most loved journals including the *Sol Plaatje European Union Anthology*, 4th edition of *Imbiza Journal* & *Fundza Literacy*. Her visualised projects on her YouTube channel have been screened on few workshops and channels including the Durban Business Fair 2021 & 1KZN TV.

Nangamso Malu is a BEd student at Walter Sisulu University. Born and raised in the Eastern Cape, she is a poet and the author of short stories.

Susan Clare Mann grew up in Durban before moving to Cape Town in 2000. She has taught part-time at the University of Cape Town since 2002, after completing an MA in Creative Writing. Her first novel, *One Tongue Singing* (2004) was shortlisted for the *Sunday Times* fiction award and translated into French and Swedish. Her second, *Quarter Tones* (2007) was shortlisted for the Commonwealth prize. She is interested in themes of belonging, nature and the role of creativity. She lives in Cape Town with her husband, three large cats and a dog.

Norman Marapo is a writer and a poet from Kroonstad in the Free State. A writer from his teens, he has been part of a local arts and writers' group in an effort to expand his knowledge of creative writing. He has written and performed many poems, and several fantasy, horror and science fiction stories, though unpublished.

Marieta McGrath holds a PhD in Molecular Biology from Stellenbosch University. From 2019 to 2021 she was the winner of several poetry competitions hosted by Litnet, the Bloemfontein Writers' Association, Minimal Press and Versindaba. *New Contrast* published three of her poems in their Summer 2021 edition. Her poems were also included in several anthologies or zines, such as *Maskers en Mure* and *Ons Klyntji*. In addition to poetry, she writes children's books of which her first was published in 2021. She lives in Somerset West.

Based in Johannesburg, **Frank Meintjies** has worked in the field of social development. He runs workshops for youth on short story and poetry writing. Frank's work has been included in several South African anthologies. Frank has also written on culture and the role of the arts in social transformation. In 2020, reflecting on Covid times, Frank has produced a collection of poetry titled *Lockdown Poems*.

Phindile Memani is currently Senior Librarian at Sir Lowry's Pass Library. His Xhosa novels *Incindi Encangathi* and *Emhadini Wemigulukudu* were published in 2012 and 2021.

Tlotisang David Mhlambiso was born in 2000 in the Western Cape, but was raised in Lugcadweni village in the Eastern Cape. He matriculated in 2018 and is currently studying Bachelor of Education majoring in English and Psychology at the University of the Free State, and forms part of the academic support staff as a teaching assistant. He is a published poet of a book entitled *Ukuphuma Kwelanga* and a short story writer in Xhosa and English.

Lindani Vitalic Mkhwana, known in the KwaZulu-Natal poetry community as Nkanyamba, is a poet, writer and performer from UMzimkhulu. Nkanyamba started writing in 2011. His love for language (especially Zulu) is seen through the diction in his poems which takes you back to the olden days of Ntu. Mkhwana is a Deputy Secretary at the UMzimkhulu Poetry Movement and he attends Loba Mentorship Program curated by IKhambi Writers Hub.

Hlengiwe Mnyandu was born in Umlazi, south of Durban, but spent most of her young life at Inanda, north of Durban. Shembe Primary School at Inanda is where she did grades 4 to 7. Her love for writing started there, she would use it as an escape and write about the future she longed for. Raised by a single mother, grandmother and uncles, she loved fairytales and still does.

Charity Baphakamile Mnyandu was born in Engonyameni, south of Durban. She attended KwaShembe primary school in Inanda and Zwelibanzi high school in Umlazi. She enjoys listening to music and reading books and newspapers. She is also very passionate about reading and writing poetry as it can relate to daily life experiences.

Mmabore Gladys Mogashoa is a heritage activist from Ga-Mogashoa village in Sekhukhune, Limpopo. She uses her talent and indigenous knowledge in poetry writing and music. She is the author of a Sepedi book titled *Bohwa bja rena*, which explores the Sepedi language and its roots, and ways of living and culture of Bapedi people. She has won several awards including the 2022 PANSALB Award, Golden Shield Heritage Awards, APAPA Award, MTCMA, Skeem Local Music awards, National Heritage Council (SA) and 2nd place at the European Union Sol Plaatje Poetry Awards 2021.

Rebaora Boitumelo Reginah Morule was born in 1999 at Itsoseng township. A poet, performer, actress, writer, author of *Ladies Talk* and motivational speaker, she worked with Atamelang Community Arts Centre. She started writing poems at 15.

Choice Dimakatso Mpanza was born and grew up at Ozwathini, in a village called Noodsberg. She has a doctorate in General Linguistics and works as a senior lecturer in the Department of English Studies at the University of South Africa. She is passionate about the development of indigenous African languages into languages that can be effectively used for teaching and learning. She loves writing about her personal experiences and observations and has recently published a collection of Zulu poems titled Imizwa nemicabango. She is also a qualified translator who translates between English and Zulu.

Simphiwe Mthombeni is a self-proclaimed night owl who writes sporadically. She was born in Mpumalanga province, stayed there for 10 years then relocated with her parents to Gauteng. When she won her first award for public speaking in 2015, she discovered her love for writing speeches and her desire in finding out ways on how to write a poem. She finally wrote her first poem titled 'Living with depression and anxiety' in 2016. She obtained a Certificate in Radio (broadcast and podcast) from AFDA and intends to study law at Unisa. She hopes and prays that one day her voice will reach thousands of ears through poetry.

Madoda Ndlakuse is a Mdantsane-born, Gqeberha-bred storyteller, poet, writer, literacy promotion and reading initiatives activist. He is passionate about reading for enjoyment and spends a lot of time helping community members, particularly children, to learn from their own stories. He works for Nalibali as a VW Project Coordinator. He is an author of a children's book called *Umtshato WeNtlanzi Nenkukhu*, poetry collections: *Iingcinga zendoda, Izitshanguba Zentlalo* and *Chuu ngcembe ngemibongo,* and is a founder of Eastern Cape Book Festival. He is a ontributing author to the Life Righting Collective's *This Is How It Is* anthology. He is a 2021 SALA winner on Nadine Gordimer Short Story category for *Mhla latsh' iBhayi*. He is the 2021/22 PanSALB Multilingualism Award winner on Xhosa.

Ongeziwe Onge Ndlangisa is a professional soccer player and holds a Diploma in Sport Management. She has recently discovered herself as a poet, and was inspired by her uncle, Kwazi Ndlangisa, who is a renowned poet in South Africa and abroad. Ndlangisa's poems steam from her questions about the upbringing of an African child in broken families as well as stories of people from her rural town, UMzimkhulu, KwaZulu-Natal.

Thalente Ndlovu is a Master's candidate at the University of KwaZulu-Natal (UKZN). She is an artist primarily practising through live performance and has recently debuted in film through the Fukamisa Intsha Film Project of UKZN. She is a published writer and poet with contributions in *Dwelling*, a limited edition printed collection of South African fine art and literature. She also contributed towards *IMBIZA Journal* in 2021.

Lesego Nkosi is a research and engagement intern at the Centre for the Advancement of Non-Racialism and Democracy at Nelson Mandela University. She is currently pursuing an Honour's degree in Sociology at Nelson Mandela University. She holds a BA in Psychology and Sociology from Nelson Mandela University and is a member of the Golden Key International Honours Society. In 2020, Lesego held a fellowship with the Democracy Works Academy (in partnership with the In Transformation Initiative). As a member of the Global Shapers Community Tshwane Hub from 2020 to 2022, she is part of several working groups engaged in conversations and solutions for a better world. As a social activist, she is greatly interested in education, mental health, and self-development to improve human rights accountability.

Ntobeko Lethu Nkwanyana is a poet and playwright. He is the founder of Let The Poet Speak Annual Poetry Show and Let The Poet Slam.

Slindile Nqashi is a BA Communication student at North West University. From KwaZulu-Natal, she was raised by a single mother. She loves reading and writing poems, and has aspirations of being an editor or journalist one day.

Zukiswa Zuki Pakama is a journalism graduate and an award-winning author who writes youth and children's novels in her mother tongue, Xhosa, and English. She has published six books in Xhosa of which four have won awards between 2013 and 2017. She has worked as a researcher, language adviser and translator for various documentary films all over the country. She is a freelance writer and some of her short stories can be found on the FunDza Literacy Trust Fund website. She also writes drama serials in Xhosa which are broadcasted by Umhlobo Wenene FM (SABC) of which the last one entitled *Inene aphel'emqaleni* was aired in April 2021. She has her poems in the *Sol Plaatje Poetry Anthology Vol IX*. She is currently busy developing a telenovela script and running a children's reading club in her community.

Hans Pienaar writes novels, plays and poetry in Afrikaans and English. He was a director of the anti-apartheid publisher Taurus and news editor of *Vrye Weekblad*, and reported for ten years on the rest of Africa and elsewhere. He won a Cosaw Short Story Prize for *My Dog Hitler*, the *Rapport* Prize for Non-Fiction for *The Third War Against Mapoch* and the national Pansa Prize for theatre texts for *Three Dozen Roses*. He is a former chairman of the Melville

Poetry Festival and has lectured in journalism at the University of Pretoria. His latest novel is *Kaap* and latest poetry collection *The Fall*.

Ferdie Robert Schaller has a background in education. He is concerned with individuals caught in events beyond their control, and how they, and the people who can influence these events, react. Poets can be neither apolitical nor neutral. He has been described by his long-suffering wife as a retreaded geographer masquerading as a poet.

Bongeka Buhle Selepe is a researcher and lecturer at the University of the Witwatersrand. In her private capacity, she works as a translator, interpreter, editor, proofreader (English/Zulu) and writer. Dr Hlengwa-Selepe is passionate about promoting Zulu as a language and does that through writing in Zulu and translating texts from English into Zulu.
Moses Seletiša is a Sepedi performance poet, translator and author. He is from Ga-Matlala' Rakgwadi in rural Limpopo. He is the author of *Tšhutšhumakgala: biography of Cde Tlokwe Maserumule, Ke Hwa Natšo* and *Re Batho le Mmino* poetry anthology.

Kagiso Sejamoholo is a poet and painter who grew up in Wolmaransstad. He started writing in 2016 after noticing how skilful he was when painting pictures with words. In 2018 he reached a milestone of 500 poems and still continues writing more English and Setswana poems.

Kagiso is studying for a Bachelor's degree in Education at Sol Plaatje University.

Siwaphiwe Fortune Shweni is from Engcobo in the Eastern Cape. He is an award-winning poet who writes mainly in Xhosa. His work has appeared in *McGregor Poetry Festival anthology* (2016), *Prufrock Magazine* (2017), AVBOB Poetry anthologies (vols 1, 2, 3), *Sol Plaatje EU anthologies* (vols 8, 9, 10) and *New Contrast*.

Sithembiso Sibisi is a creative person who started writing at the age of 13 and has self-published two books. Sithembiso believes in creating opportunities instead of waiting for others to open doors for him. His unique ability to work well with people has seen him holding positions that others think are meant for certain people. Once he has set his eyes on something, he goes all out to get it and he makes sure that he excels in it.

Petros Sipho was born in Eutreght in 1978 and grew up with his grandmother in Clera Farm, Dannhauser, KwaZulu-Natal.

Lazola Leon Sukula is a South African poet, writer and publisher. His work is published in Zimbabwe, Nigeria, Ireland, Singapore, Canada, India and United States of America. He writes both in English and Zulu. He lives in Emalahleni, Kwa-guqa, Mpumalanga Province.

Jarred James Thompson is a literary and cultural studies researcher based in Johannesburg, South Africa. His fiction has been published in the *Johannesburg Review of Books*, *FIYAH* and *The Gerald Kraak Award Anthology* (2019). He is the winner of the 2020 Afritondo Short Story Prize. He is also the second place winner of the 2021 Dream Foundry Short Story Prize. His debut novel, *The Institute for Creative*

Dying, is forthcoming from Afritondo UK Press and Picador Africa. He currently lectures in the English Department at the University of Pretoria, where he is completing his PhD.

Mbulelo Tshofela was born in Mdantsane Township. He grew up in Nonibe and Bozwana villages in Eastern Cape. He's the motivational speaker, spiritual life coach and consultant. He's the author of two self-published books *Only Through the Desert* and *I Rise.* He holds a National Diploma: Internal Auditing from Nelson Mandela University and Post Graduate Diploma: Leadership Development from Stellenbosch University. He's the owner of Bavuse Consulting, a company specialising in Strategy, Risk and Performance Management. Personal leadership and writing and reading fascinates him.

Crystal Warren is a South African poet and children's author who has lived and worked in the Eastern Cape her whole life. She grew up in Gqebeha (formerly Port Elizabeth) and lives in Makhanda (formerly Grahamstown). Her poems have been published in numerous journals and anthologies and in two collections: Bodies of Glass (Aerial Publishing) and Predictive Text (Modjaji Books). She edited New Coin Poetry for four years, teaches creative writing workshops, and is one of the coordinators and hosts of Makhanda monthly open mic Reddit's Poetry.

Zusakhe Rhasatsha Zide is an award-winning poet, who realized her artistic abilities in Umtata in her teen years doing monologues with the WSU theatre production. She was born in Port Elizabeth in 2002.

Nkululeko Zondi is an HIV/Aids educator at the City of Johannesburg Municipality and an occupational journalism student at the Fray College of Communications. A former student of the University of Johannesburg, he holds a liberal arts degree from the University of South Africa. He writes poetry and prose in both Zulu and English, and has been published in numerous online literary publications. Recently, Zondi became second-prize winner in both AVBOB Poetry's Ecopoetry mini-competition in April 2022 and AVBOB Poetry's Family First mini-competition in May 2022.

Lucas Delisiwe Zulu is a South African poet, writer and publisher. His work is published in Zimbabwe, Nigeria, Ireland, Singapore, Canada, India, United States of America. He writes both in English and Zulu. He lives in Emalahleni, Kwa-guqa, Mpumalanga Province.

What is the European Union (EU)?

The European Union is a unique economic and political union between 27 European countries[1] that together cover much of the European continent. The EU was created in the aftermath of World War II. The first steps were to foster economic cooperation: the idea being that countries that trade with one another become economically interdependent and so more likely to avoid conflict.

Since its birth, the union has developed into a single market with the euro (€) as its common currency. What began as a purely economic union has evolved into an organisation spanning policy areas from external relations and security, justice and migration to health, environment and climate. With the global Covid-19 pandemic, Green Recovery has taken centre stage.

The single or "internal" market is the EU's main economic engine, enabling most goods, services, money and people to move freely. Another key objective is to develop this huge resource also in other areas like energy, knowledge and capital markets to ensure that its citizens can draw the maximum benefit from it.

The EU is based on the rule of law: everything it does is founded on treaties, voluntarily and democratically agreed by its member countries. It actively promotes human rights and democracy and in 2012 was awarded the Nobel Peace Prize for advancing the causes of peace, reconciliation, democracy and human rights in Europe.

---

1   At the time of writing: Belgium, Bulgaria, Croatia, Czech Republic, Denmark, Germany, Estonia, Ireland, Greece, Spain, France, Italy, Cyprus, Latvia, Lithuania, Luxembourg, Hungary, Malta, the Netherlands, Austria, Poland, Portugal, Romania, Slovenia, Slovakia, Finland, and Sweden.

How does it work?
EU Member States have set up institutions to run the EU and adopt its legislation. The main ones are:
- The European Parliament (representing the people of Europe)
- The Council of the European Union (representing national governments)
- The European Commission (representing the common EU interest)

Size and population
The EU is less than half the size of the United States covering some 4 million square kilometres. In terms of size, France is the EU's largest country and Malta its smallest. The EU has a population of close to 450 million people – the world's third largest after China and India.

EU symbols
- The European flag: the 12 stars in a circle symbolise the ideals of unity, solidarity and harmony among the peoples of Europe.
- The European anthem: the melody used to symbolise the EU comes from Ludwig Van Beethoven's 9th Symphony composed in 1823.
- Europe Day: the ideas behind the EU were first put forward on 9 May 1950 by French Foreign Minister Robert Schuman. This is why 9 May is celebrated as a key date for the EU.
- The EU motto: "United in diversity".

The EU's economy
Operating as a single market, the EU is a major world trading power. The EU's unique social market economy

allows its economies to grow and to reduce poverty and inequality. EU economic policy focuses on creating jobs and boosting growth by making smarter use of financial resources, removing obstacles to investment and providing visibility and technical assistance to investment projects. Small- and medium-sized enterprises form the backbone of the EU's economy.

The EU & South Africa: A partnership of equals

Since 1994 the growing relationship between South Africa and the EU has been underpinned by the Trade, Development and Cooperation Agreement (TDCA). Closer ties between the two parties were consolidated in 2007 with the establishment of the EU–SA Strategic Partnership. This partnership, the only one of its kind with an African country, is centred on enhanced political dialogue around issues of shared interest including climate change, the global economy, governance, bilateral trade, and peace and security matters. In line with this, its action plan encompasses sectoral cooperation on a range of issues such as climate change, environment, education, science and technology, space, trade and migration. Regular high level meetings steer the partnership, along with the EU-South Africa Joint Cooperation Council. They provide the occasions to discuss current bilateral, regional and global issues.

Trade & investment

The EU is not only South Africa's biggest trading partner but remains its dominant source of foreign direct investment stock (40.3%). EU generated investments have created in excess of 350,000 direct jobs. South Africa's total trade with the EU is in the region of €40 billion. More importantly,

55% of South Africa's exports to the EU consist of agri-food and manufactured goods, which contribute directly to beneficiation and employment and thus to inclusive growth. The entry into force of the SADC–EU Economic Partnership Agreement is generating new opportunities to further strengthen bilateral trade and investment relations.

Development cooperation
The bilateral EU cooperation programme in South Africa provides support to the value of €281 million with additional funding being channelled for thematic focus areas in the form of grants. In addition to that, the total official support of the EU to sustainable development in South Africa includes programmes such as the Erasmus+ programme, and joint EU-South Africa Science and Innovation cooperation through the European Commission's Horizon 2020 Programme. The European Investment Bank makes available some €462 million in long-term loans and there are significant bilateral cooperation programmes between EU Member States and South Africa.